THE LIFE AND SPORT OF THE INN

THE LIFE AND SPORT OF THE INN

MICHAEL BRANDER

GENTRY BOOKS : LONDON

First published 1973

ISBN 0 85614 0252

Published by
Gentry Books Limited
15, Tooks Court,
London EC4A 1LA

Layout and Design Brian Roll

Printed by Ebenezer Baylis and Son Limited
The Trinity Press, Worcester, and London

To Beb who likes Scotch whisky and Leo who likes Irish

Contents

Illustrations to Chapter Headings

Illustrations

Acknowledgements

Since no-one has previously covered this particular rather wide field I must acknowledge at once that I am entirely responsible for any mistakes or errors, of omission or commission.

My thanks for their assistance are due to The Brewers' Society, particularly Mr. A. T. E. Binstead, also the National Federation of Licensed Victuallers and their Secretary, Mr. A. Boardman. The following individual Brewers in particular: Messrs. Allied Breweries, Bass-Charrington, Courage, Scottish and Newcastle Breweries, John Smith's Tadcaster Brewery Company, Watney Mann, Whitbreads, Vaux.

Author's Preface

TO WRITE ABOUT English Inns without writing about drink and drinking seems to me arid nonsense. Yet, when writing about inns and drinking, how can one leave out the sports and pastimes which go with them? Very clearly they are virtually indivisible. Men, and women too, have always gone to alehouses, inns and taverns to drink and disport themselves with gaiety, games, gossip and song. They still do and doubtless in the years to come they still will. At least it is to be sincerely hoped they will, for once the custom ceases something vitally important will have gone out of the national life.

Although there have been books on the history of inns and others on the history of drink and drinking and yet others on sports and pastimes, there has never previously been an attempt to trace the inter-relationship between the three. Of course, when tracing the development of alehouses, inns and taverns as well as the drinks and entertainments provided over the centuries, mention must be made of the changes affecting brewers, distillers, vintners, innkeepers, ostlers and others associated with them. Such inter-related features as new methods of travel, the growth of tea and coffee drinking and of the temperance movement must be included. The reasons for the contrasting growth of the Highland Inn have also to be considered. So vast a field can only be lightly covered within the scope of this book, but, as far as possible, commentators in each century have been allowed to make their points for themselves, since these are subjects on which people have always held decided views.

It is not often an author can truthfully say the subject matter of a book has been a lifetime's study, but that is very nearly true in this instance. It is one I have always found of absorbing interest. Tracing the development of alehouses, inns and taverns and their manifold ancillaries has been an enjoyable disport in itself. It is to be hoped that the reader will also find it rewarding and enjoyable.

Chapter One

Drink and Disport

Past thousand years – Origins of Ale in Persia – Pliny the Elder not approving – Celts reasons for drinking – King Edgar's Archbishop decree against drinking – On Wakes – Ales another form of feast – Cause of drunkenness – Decrees on sport – Prohibited sports under Edward III – Wine drinking – Introduction of Beer. Andrew Boorde on Ale and Beer Distillation – Peter Morwyng – Sack, or Sherry – Sports – Stubbs on Maypole – Origins of Gin – William Vaughan on Wine – Gervase Markham on Claret – Burton on Games – John Taylor – Stingo, Nipitatum

If all be true that I do think,
There are five reasons we should drink,
Good wine – a friend – or being dry,
Or lest we should be by and by,
Or any other reason why.

HENRY ALDRICH, Dean of Christchurch: 1648–1710.

OVER THE CENTURIES in Britain men particularly and women to a lesser degree have disported themselves in alehouses, inns and taverns with conversation and song, with cards and dice and similar games of chance or skill, also with ball games and more strenuous pursuits outdoors. All these disports and the inns themselves have developed over the past thousand years or more with the habit of drinking and have to a considerable degree mirrored the age. Essentially, therefore, this is a book about the changing drinking habits of the country, whether affected by new laws, by the introduction of new forms of drink, such as tea or cheap gin, by new forms of transport, such as the canals or the stage-coach, by new forms of communication, such as the radio or television, or by internal, or external convulsions, such as the Civil War or the 1914–1918 War, which basically affected the ingrained habits of centuries.

As long ago as 5,000 B.C. the Persians knew how to ferment barley and the Egyptians depicted the entire process of brewing. Indeed it is almost certainly from these regions that the earliest barley grown in Britain was obtained. From various pottery remains it is known that barley was cultivated in Britain around 3,000 B.C. and it may safely be assumed that the knowledge of how to brew it into an intoxicating drink had accompanied the seed. By the time the Romans, under Julius Caesar, invaded Britain in 55 B.C. the cultivation of barley was widespread and no doubt ale was produced from it almost everywhere. Although cider, mead and even imported wines may have been drunk in some areas, ale was undoubtedly the most common drink in the country. Pliny the Elder recorded disapprovingly:

'The natives who inhabit the west of Europe have a liquid with which they intoxicate themselves made from corn and water . . . So exquisite is the cunning of mankind in gratifying their vicious appetites that they have thus invented a method to make water itself produce intoxication.'

Pliny, of course, lived in a warm climate and he had the civilised Roman's contempt for barbarian practices. When grapes were available to produce wine it would have been superfluous to produce alcohol by any other means. Heating barley in water and fermenting the ensuing brew to produce a probably rather unpleasant tasting primitive ale, or barley wine, may have seemed unnecessary to him, but he did not live in these chilly, rainswept islands.

It was precisely because ale warmed their bellies and raised their spirits that the primitive Celts appreciated it and their more advanced Anglo-Saxon supplanters after them. They had little enough to break the monotony of their lives, unless it was the prospect of fighting to preserve them. From the earliest records conversation and song appear to have been the invariable accompaniment of their ale drinking and to have ranked amongst their chief amusements. Before the days of the printed word and widespread literacy, the story-teller and the rhymester were the chief entertainers in the alehouses. Songs and choruses also seem to have been a recognised form of alehouse merriment.

During the reign of King Edgar (957–975) Archbishop Dunstan decreed that:

'No priest be an ale-scop (i.e. a reciter in an alehouse) nor in any wise act the gleeman.'

From this it would seem plain that even at such an early date singing in alehouses was a well established custom. A recognisable picture emerges, for in those days under the Saxon kings hunting was a dangerous sport and it was the custom for the hounds to be trencher fed; that is, each hound being kept and looked after by a separate villager, freeman or bondman. On the day of the hunt they would be called together and the hounds hunted in couples or individually in pursuit of deer, wild boar and wolves. It is easy to imagine how satisfactory it must have been for the returned villagers to relax in the alehouse afterwards. As they felt the strong ale warming their bodies and easing the tensions of the day no doubt they boasted of the narrow escapes they had had and sang of the beasts they had killed.

It is significant that another of the decrees issued in King Edgar's reign related to Wakes. These were religious ceremonies of thanksgiving held on the anniversary of the dedication of a church, or on the saint's day to which it was consecrated. Through the night prior to the ceremony the people were expected to hold a fasting vigil in small tents or booths set up near the church. In the early days of the Church these occasions appear to have had a certain pagan significance and after the ceremony the people gave themselves up to feasting and ale-drinking. The decree ordered those attending a Wake 'to pray devoutly and not betake themselves to drunkenness and debauchery'.

An early author described the scene after a Wake as follows:

'And afterwards the pepul fell to letcherie and songs and daunces with harping and piping, and also to glotony and sinne . . .'

Understandably, such feasts were popular and similar regular feasts, known as church ales, were held annually, generally at Christmas, Easter and Whitsun, with a view to raising money for the upkeep of the church. Prior to these the churchwardens or parish officers brewed a quantity of strong ale from barley provided by the parishioners. This was then sold to those attending the feast and the proceeds went to the church funds in the same way as the modern coffee morning, or church bazaar, of which these were the forerunners.

The secular equivalent of the church ale was known as a scot ale. Scot was a corruption of the Saxon word 'sceat' meaning a part, so that a scot ale was literally a feast at which everyone had provided a part. Originally the stewards or bailiffs collected a part of each man's harvest and brewed ale from it which was then sold at the scot ale. Latterly the term scot ale seems to have been used loosely to describe any gathering of ten or more who had provided their own ale and scot ales were thus the equivalent of the modern bottle party. There were also numerous other excuses for ales, such as bride ales, weddyn ales, midsummer ales, lamb ales and tithe ales, to name but a few.

Some of these early feasts, particularly the Wakes, continued as late as the 19th century and several, of course, still have their modern counterparts. The scot ales, however, proved a continual source of trouble from an early date, initially due to the opportunities they provided for extortion by unscrupulous minor officials enforcing contributions from those beneath them, and latterly because they were the cause of so much drunkenness. The Church, in particular, issued repeated decrees against them, but their very repetition indicates their ineffectiveness.

Another decree issued in King Edgar's reign forbade a priest to hunt, hawk or dice, from which it may be inferred that they frequently indulged in all three and that it was felt these pursuits should be reserved for the nobility. Subsequent decrees of a similar nature were repeated and as late as 1240 in the reign of Henry III priests were forbidden to play cards or dice. Once again the continual repetition of such orders in itself underlines how consistently they were being ignored.

It was not until 1326 in the reign of Edward III that an Act was passed making illegal a number of pursuits, which it was claimed were distracting his subjects from practising archery and martial exercises. These illegal games included cards, dice, games of chance, throwing at stones, wood or iron, football, handball, club-ball and cambucam (played with a curved stick and said to be the forerunner of hockey), while bull-baiting and cock-fighting were specifically condemned as worthless sports. In subsequent Acts, quoits and kayles, or ninepins, were added to the list. The probability is that few, if any, of these Acts were very effective deterrents, but they indicate the popular games of the day. It is the way of bureaucracy in any Age that as late as the reign of Henry VIII, when archery had almost ceased to have any real significance, a final Act added bowling and 'playing at tables', or backgammon, to the list. By that time the law was probably being freely broken in most alehouses, inns and taverns in the land.

It must be remembered that the Normans were principally wine

A 14th-century tavern and cellar

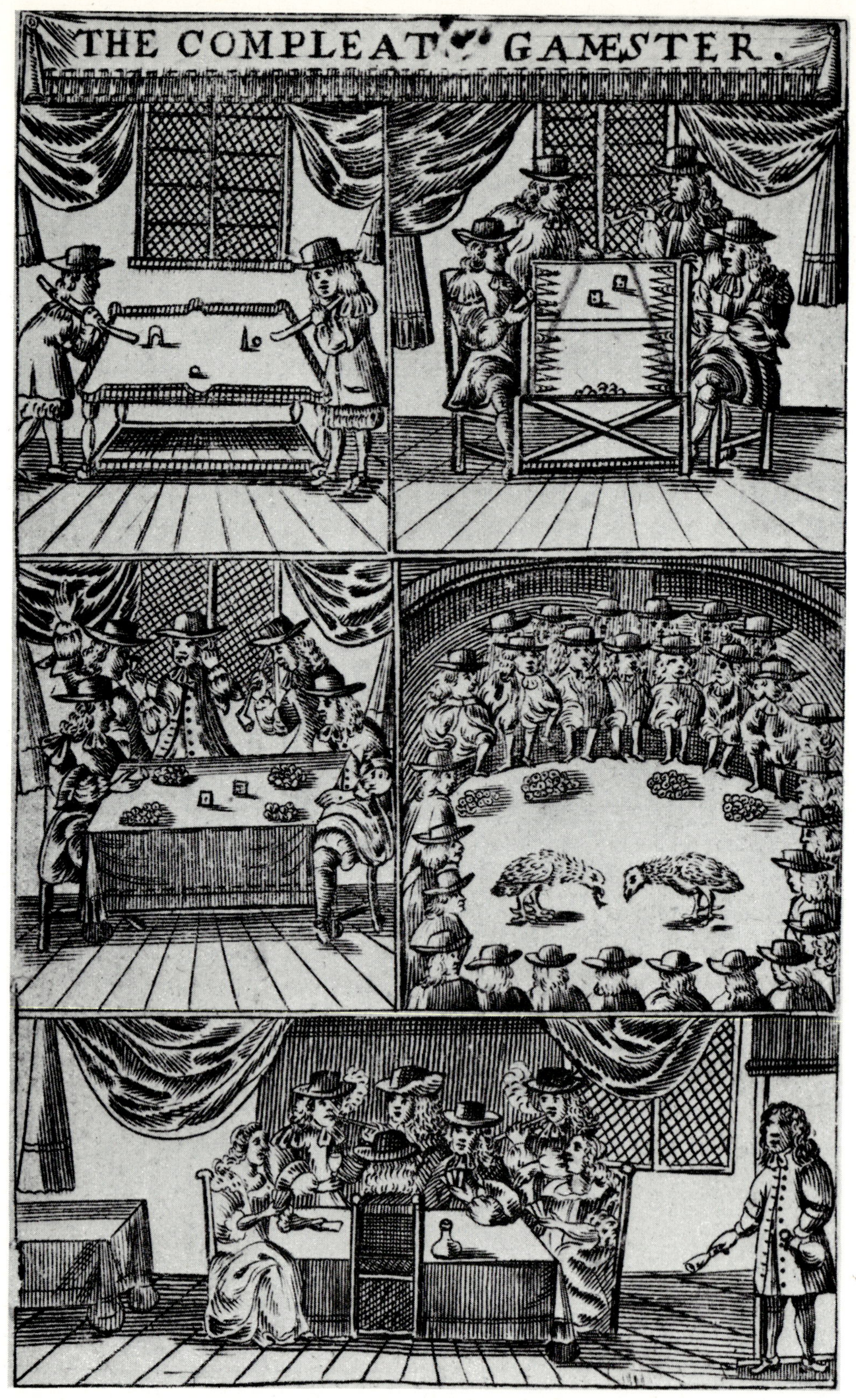

Billiards, backgammon, dice, cock-fighting and basset

drinkers. Although as many as thirty-eight vineyards are listed in the Domesday Book survey of 1087 and although the ale produced in the English monasteries was already famed on the Continent, it may therefore be assumed that from the Norman Conquest onwards the demand for wine increased. With the marriage of Henry II in 1159 to Eleanor of Aquitaine, wine from the lands around Bordeaux was as readily available as ale and entered the country in enormous quantities, duty free, until the end of the Hundred Years War in 1453. Throughout the later Middle Ages both ale and wine were readily obtainable in England.

Of course at this period each alehouse and inn brewed its own ale, as did each household of any size, producing immensely varied results, but at its best a strong, clear rather sweet tasting brew. It was not until the start of the 15th century when hops were first introduced from Holland that the more bitter tasting beer began gradually to become popular. In England, originally, ale and beer had been two names for the same, or a similar, drink, the word ale being commonly used by the Danes in the east and beer by the Saxons in the west. With the Norman Conquest the old Saxon term was dropped until introduced again from Holland along with the hop. By this time the original usage had been forgotten and the new brew met with considerable opposition in many quarters. The change-over to beer as the national drink was not effected without a good deal of dissension over the next hundred-and-fifty years or more.

In 1542 we find Andrew Boorde in his *Dyetary of Health* writing on the subject of Beer:

'Bere is made of malte, of hoppes and water; it is the naturall drynke for a Dutche man and now of late dayes it is much used in England to the detryment of many Englyshe people; specyally it killeth them which be troubled with the colyke, and the stone and the strangulation; for the drynke is a cold drynke; yet it doth make a man fat, and doth inflate the bely, as it doth appere by the Dutchemen's faces and belyes. If the bere be well served and be fyned, and not new it doth qualify heat of the lyver.'

On Ale he was most emphatic:

'Ale is for an Englyshe man a natural drynke. Ale must have these properties; it must be freshe and cleare, it must not be ropy nor smoky. Ale should not be dranke under five days olde. Newe ale is unwholsome for all men. And soure ale, and deade ale which doth stand a-tilt is good for no man. Barley malte maketh better ale than oten malte or any other corne doth; it doth ingendre grose humoures; but yet it maketh a man strong.'

During the 16th century the Reformation saw the spread of many new ideas in spheres other than Religion and the Arts, not least on the subject of drink. Although distillation is thought to have originated in the East around 2000 B.C., or even earlier, it did not reach Europe until the 12th century and was not common until the 15th century. The earliest description of the methods involved, written in English, is contained in the translation of a book by Jerome Braunschweig published in 1525 and entitled *The Virtuose Boke of Distyllacyon.* Previously prized as a love potion and aphrodisiac, in this work Aqua Vitae is treated as a medicine to be taken, a few drops at a time, in a glass of wine. This state of affairs did not last long once the taste was acquired, although considering that it was often made from the dregs of sour wine or ale and the fact that little or no flavouring was used, the taste must have been particularly unpleasant.

In 1559 Peter Morwyng published his *Treasure of Evonymous,* which dealt with the subject more fully. Arguing that it did not matter whether spirits were distilled from good wine or from bad wine, or the lees of wine, he maintained that: 'if it be distilled often it shal be made the more effectuall, hotter and drier.'

He went on to point out the benefits of Aqua Vitae in a manner reminiscent of the salesman of patent medicines:

'It helpeth red and duskish eyes. It is good for them that have the falling sickness if they drink it. It cureth the palsy if they be onoynted therewith. It sharpeneth the wit, it restoreth memori. It maketh men merry and preserveth youth. It putteth away fracins, ring worms and all spots of the face, etc. It is merveylous profitable for frantic men and such as be melancoly. It expelleth poison. The smell thereof burnt, killeth flies and cold creeping beasts. It restoreth wine that is turned or putrefied.

'It is most wholesome for the stomake, the harte and the liver; it nourisheth blood; it agreeth merveylously and most with men's nature . . . it taketh away sadness, pensiveness; it maketh men merri, witti and encreaseth audacitie.'

Peter Morwyng also commented on another feature of the period, namely the addition of spices to wines. He noted: 'Raspish wyne, that whych biteth the tong with a certayn sharp biting, it provoketh appetite, bindyng the heates of the stomach . . . Some put spices also to the raspish wyne as galangal five ounces, cinamon, cloves, of either two ounces, etc.'

Another introduction in the 1530s which was to grow extremely popular by the turn of the century was Sack – at first spelled Seck – or Sherry, from Spain, described as a dry, yellowish wine. It was often sweetened with sugar by taverners and it was common practice to add spices, eggs, or toast to it. Like all wines in Tudor times and earlier, it was drunk young, within six months to a year at the latest, before it had turned to vinegar in the imperfectly sealed casks of the times. The same applied to the other wines available, the Bordeaux wines, white and red, the claret, the malmsey, muscadel, and the Rhenish wines imported through Holland to Deal. Although there were an increasing variety of wines and other drinks available in Tudor times, they were mostly young and robust. In many ways it was a young and robust age, above all lusty and vigorous.

Their amusements, and their humour, reflected this vigour. Hunting the hart, the buck and the hare, as well as falconry, were still principally the sports of the aristocracy. Although jousting was out-moded, tilting at the quintain, a target on a pivot, which swung round and buffeted the unwary, wrestling, vieing with quarter staves until the blood ran from their heads, archery, football, handball, or fives, bowls, quoits, skittles and cock-fighting were among the commonest pursuits. Brutish pastimes such as bear- and bull-baiting with dogs, or throwing sticks at tethered cocks were also frequently practised. Dancing round the village maypole may, or may not, have been a comparatively innocuous pastime, but pelting the wretches in the stocks or the pillories was a cruder form of amusement.

Even that bigotted Tudor Puritan, Philip Stubbs writing in 1583 in his *Anatomie of Abuses*, could not help giving a rather attractive picture of the May Day celebrations, although far from his intention:

'Against Maie-day . . . all the young men and maides, old men and wives, run gadding overnight to the woods, groves, hills and mountains, where they spend all the night in pleasant pastimes and in the morning they return bringing with them birche boughes and branches of trees to deck their assemblies withal. But their chiefest jewel they bring from thence is the Maie-pole, which they bring home with great veneration, as thus – they have twentie or fourtie yoake of oxen, every oxe having a sweete nosegaie of flowers tied to the tip of his hornes, and these oxen drawe home the May-poale, their stinking idol rather, which they covered all over with flowers and hearbes, bound round with strings from the top to the bottome, and sometimes it was painted with variable colours, having two or three hundred men, women and children following it with great devotion. And thus equipped it was reared with handkerchiefs and flagges streaming on the top, they strawe the ground round about it, they bind green boughs about it, they set up summer halles, bowers and arbours hard by it, and then fall they to banquetting and feasting, to leaping and dauncing about it, as the heathen people did at the dedication of their idolls. I have heard it crediblie reported, by men of great gravity, credite, and reputation, that of fourtie, threescore, or an hundred maides going to the wood, there have scarcely the third part of them returned home againe as they went.'

To gain a lifting of their spirits and an increase in mental and bodily activity, or simply to quench their thirsts, they drank both ale and wine freely, while they engaged in such pursuits, or while they relaxed, telling stories, singing choruses, or watching itinerant players, jugglers, acrobats or similar entertainers. Drunkards were liable to end up in the stocks, but drinking was a subject for mirth rather than for social or moral censure. Yet towards the end of the century tastes were changing.

The popular saying then was 'Drunk as a Dutchman' and not without reason. When an expedition led by Leicester was sent to the Netherlands in 1586, they returned with an acquired taste for spirits. The Dutch name for juniper berries, with which their spirits were flavoured, was Genever, soon shortened to Geneva and thence to Gin. It was from this time that the demand for spirits amongst all classes of society first became general. The immediate consequence was that the standard of the spirits being produced sank even lower and they were being distilled from all sorts of highly undesirable sources. Nor at this period, was there any check on the methods of distillation.

By this time Sack was well established, but in 1600 William Vaughan wrote in his *Directions for Health, naturall and artificiall*:

'Sacke doth make men fat and foggy, and therefore is not to be taken of young men. Being drunke before supper with a store of sugar, it provoketh appetite, comforteth the spirits marvellously and concocteth raw humours. Canary Sacke is more full of spirits than any other.'

Concerning 'Muscadell, Malmesie and Brown Bastard' he recorded rather obscurely:

'These kind of wines are only for married folkes, because they strengthen the backs, yet I wish them to be very chary in the drinking thereof, lest their often use fill the veines and seede vessells with unnatural accidental windy puft . . . But for aged persons, these high and yellowish wines are wonderfull wholesome in the winter time.'

On the subject of beer and ale he demonstrated that the prejudice against beer was now virtually a thing of the past and also indicated a reason why ale had lost some of its popularity:

'Beere which is made of good Malt, well brewed, not too new nor too stale, nourisheth the body, causeth a good colour, and passeth out of the body. Stale with a good store of sugar, eyther in the morning, or before meales, it rejoyceth the heart, cleareth the complexion and cureth Melancholy.

'Ale made of barley malt and good water, doth make a man strong; but nowadaies few brewers brew it as they ought; for they add slimy and heavy baggage unto it, thinking thereby to please tosse-pots, and to encrease the vigour of it. Good Ale ought to be fresh and cleare of colour. It must not be tilted, for then the best qualitie is spent; it must neither look muddy, nor yet carry a tayle with it.'

Despite the apparent caution displayed by William Vaughan, Sack, or Sherry, was accepted generally throughout the country with surprising speed. From being first introduced in the 1530s, it was being freely drunk by the end of the century. With most new drinks, as with beer and spirits, the delay in general acceptance was a full hundred years or more. Of course ale was very firmly established and apart from that England was still primarily a wine drinking country. In the 1590s around 7,000 tuns, or 28,000 hogsheads, of wine was being imported annually from Bordeaux alone, despite a tax of 40s a tun, which in those days was a considerable sum. When a commercial agreement was signed between France and England in 1606 the amount imported no doubt increased.

Of all the wines drunk in England at this time, Claret was probably the most popular. Nor, though the wines were drunk young, was there any lack of true wine expertise in choosing them. With claret this was especially the case. In 1611, in his *Country Contentments*, Gervase Markham, the celebrated Elizabethan author, explained to the English housewife how to chose her claret as follows:

'See that in your choice of Gascoine wines, you observe that your Claret wines be faire coloured, and bright as a Ruby, not deep as an Amethest; for though it may show strength, yet it wanteth neatness; also let it be sweet as a Rose, or a Violet, and in any case let it be short, for if it be too long, then in no case meddle with it.'

This was a period when fortunes were being quickly made, and sometimes as quickly lost, by merchant adventurers outfitting ships for foreign trade which returned from the East Indies laden with spices, ivory or silks, or vanished without trace. The emergent Middle Classes wished to learn how to behave in the manner suited to their wealth and there was no lack of books such as Gervase Markham's to instruct them in how to brew ale, make home-made wines, or similar arts. No doubt the alehouses, inns and taverns profited in proportion as the new found wealth entered the country.

Yet the occupations and amusements of all classes during the long, dark, winter evenings, or during the few idle moments in the heat of the summer, remained very little altered. Robert Burton in his *Anatomy of Melancholy* listed the amusements of 'greater men' as:

'Riding of great horses, running at rings, tilts and tournaments, horse-races and wild-goose-chases (i.e. follow-my-leader on horseback).' Rural recreations he included were: 'Ringing, bowling, shooting, playing with keel-pins (skittles), tronks (a form of bowls), coits, pitching of bars, hurling, wrestling, leaping, running, fencing, swimming, playing with wasters (singlesticks), foils, foot-balls, balowns, running at the quintain.' Indoor games included: 'Cards, tables, dice, shovel-board (a forerunner of shove-halfpenny), chess play, small trunks (a form of bagatelle), shuttlecock, billiards, music, masks, singing, dancing, frolicks, jests, riddles, catches, cross-purposes, questions and commands, merry tales of errant knights, queens, lovers, lords, ladies, giants, dwarfs, thieves, cheaters, witches, fairies, goblins and friars.'

Throughout most of the 17th century wine drinking, with claret perhaps the most favoured wine of all, was to reach its height. Yet as late as the 1630s John Taylor, the eccentric self-styled water poet and always, admittedly, something of a reactionary and espouser of lost causes, was referring to beer in a pamphlet entitled *Drink and Welcome* as follows:

'Now to write of Beere, I shall not need to wet my pen much with the naming of it, it being a drink which Antiquitie was an Alien or a meere stranger to, and as it hath scarcely any name, so it hath no habitation, for the places or houses where it is sold doth still retain the name of an

Alehouse . . . Beere is but an Upstart and a Foreigner or Alien in respect of Ale.'

Over two hundred years had passed and still beer was under attack, although by this time it also had its pot-valiant supporters. Yet it is understandable that drinkers of strong local ales with names such as Yorkshire Stingo, huff-cap, nipitatum, nipitato, Pharoah, Nanny Driffield's, Mother Penwaker's and many others, some of which were reputedly strong enough to burn like Sack when lit, were not easily lured from their favourite brews. The new bitter beer was an acquired taste and for another hundred years at least ale was to have its faithful devotees, although ultimately beer was to become accepted as the national drink in its place. Meanwhile, with the uncontrolled growth of spirit-drinking, the seeds of much future drunkenness and dissension were being sown.

Chapter Two

Mainly Drink

Distillers Company – Effects of Puritan Regime – Treaty with Portugal – Pepys – Tea, Coffee, Chocolate – Brandy – Free Traders – Gin Age – Figures – Legislation – Addison – Defoe – New Beers – Porter – Moritz – De la Rochefoucauld – Cock-fighting – Cobbett – Adam Smith – Duke of Wellington's Act 1830 – Phylloxera – Whisky

Beer, happy produce of our Isle,
Can sinewy strength impart
And wearied with fatigue and toil,
Can chear each manly heart.

Gin Cursed Fiend with Fury fraught,
Makes human Race a Prey:
It enters by a deadly Draught,
And steals our Life away.

From Beer Street and Gin Lane: Hogarth. ANON.

THE TIME LAG between the introduction of a new drink and its general acceptance throughout the country seems to have extended to an even greater degree to the legislation concerning drink. This was always notably behind events and few other subjects seem to have been so bedevilled by contrary and ill-advised Acts of Parliament, or other governmental action. Thus, although distilling was written about as early as 1525 and was common by the middle of the century, nothing was done to control it before 1638 and even then it was more high-sounding than effective.

In 1638, Charles I, on the advice of his physician Sir Theodore de Mayern, granted the Distillers Company their first Charter. Sir Theodore and the Queen's physician Dr. Thomas Cademan, who became the first Master of the Distillers Company, framed the regulations, which read in part:

'No Afterworts, or Wash (of brewers) called Blew John, nor musty, unsavoury of unwholesome tills, or dregs of beer or ale; nor unwholesome or adulterated wines, or Lees of wines; nor unwholesome sugar-water, musty, unsavoury, or unwholesome returned Beer or Ale; nor rotten, unsavoury or corrupt fruits, druggs, spices, herbs, seeds; nor any other ill-conditioned materials of what kind soever, shall henceforth be distilled, extracted or drawn into small spirits, or Low wines, or be in any other way used, directly or indirectly, by any of the Members of this Company, or their successors at any time hereafter for ever.'

For ever in this case was to last until the 1690s, but first came the Civil War of 1642, followed by more than a decade of Puritan rule, when the Maypoles and Church ales were abolished, public cock-fighting banned and compulsory churchgoing enforced. Even horse-racing was halted for a short period and for the first time a tax was levied on ale and beer. Despite the revulsion of feeling which followed on the Restoration of Charles II, the old gay Sunday afternoons, when the people had gathered together and disported themselves freely, were never to return. Gone, too, were the Maypoles and much of the innocent, or not so innocent amusement associated with them and despite isolated attempts to revive them, they, too, were never to return.

The dismal Sunday afternoons which the English have endured ever since were one of the permanent legacies of the Puritan regime. So, too, was the ingrained lesson that sex and drinking were shameful acts and drunkenness enough to condemn anyone to the nethermost regions. Needless to say, the knowledge only added a certain grim determination to the deed, but it effectively stifled much of the pleasure. It is not entirely fanciful to conclude that at least for a while something of the old laughter and gaiety went out of the nation to be replaced by an alien earnestness and hypocrisy. Last, but not least, in spite of expectations to the contrary, like most taxes once imposed, the tax on ale and beer remained.

The Puritans certainly left their mark. Yet the face of the countryside was changing remorselessly and, to some extent inevitably, the habits of the countryside were changing with it. The steady pace of the Enclosures was sweeping away the old open-field system of farming, and by dividing up the common land, was producing the hedgerow-patterned landscape of the Britain we know today. Ultimately the process was to pave the way for the Industrial developments of the late 18th and early 19th centuries. It produced today's familiar village green and village inn, but it also drove masses of the poor from the countryside to seek refuge in the towns and the solace of cheap gin.

From the viewpoint of many Englishmen in the years to come the one redeeming feature of the Commonwealth regime was the Commercial Treaty of 1654 signed with Portugal. The long friendship and alliance between the two countries maintained since then has its roots in this Treaty, which it must be admitted was only secured through the blockade enforced by Admiral Blake and the hard bargaining of Cromwell himself when King John IV of Portugal was in no position to argue. However it was a direct result of the establishment at that time of an autonomous body of English merchants in Portugal, who took up their residence there, that the port-wine trade of the ensuing centuries developed as it did.

Between 1650 and 1660, more appropriately during the Puritan regime, three non-alcoholic drinks, coffee, chocolate and tea, were introduced to England and were ultimately to alter the drinking habits of the nation even more than the introduction of cheap spirits. At first these innovations were restricted to the wealthy. In 1660 tea was imported through Holland and cost between £2–£3 per pound. Chocolate and coffee were also comparatively expensive at first, although in a short time coffee houses were abounding and in due course coffee rooms in inns were to follow.

In his diary for 19th June, 1660, Samuel Pepys recorded:

'When I came home I found a Quantity of Chocolate left for me, but I know not from whom.'

For 25th September, 1660, he noted:

'To the office . . . I sat a while . . . and afterwards did send for a Cupp of Tee (a China drink) of which I never drunk before.'

Another new drink of the period, which he first mentions drinking on the night before the Coronation of Charles II in April 1661, was Mum, an ale brewed with wheat in Brunswick. A description of the method of making it runs as follows:

'As soon as the beer begins to work, they put into it the inner rind of fir, tops of fir and birch, betony, marjory, pennyroyal, wild thyme, etc. Our English brewers use cardamum, ginger and sassafras instead of the inner rind of fir, and add also walnut rinds, madder, red sanders and elecampans.'

Not surprisingly, perhaps, Pepys does not seem to have drunk much of it, but he was certainly not averse to strong drink as his entries for 2nd and 3rd April, 1661, indicate clearly enough:

'2nd . . . Then to the Dolphin to Sir W. Batten and Pen and other company . . . parted all friends at twelve at night after drinking a great deal of wine. So home and alone to bed.

'3rd . . . my head akeing all day from last night's debauch . . . at noon dined with Sir W. Batten and Pen, who would needs have me drink two good draughts of Sack today to cure me of last night's disease – which I thought strange, but I think I find it true . . .'

A few years later a certain Mr. Thomas Gorway might have suggested a different cure. Among the first of the tea importers on a large scale, he was soon writing in a style curiously reminiscent of Peter Morwyng more than a century earlier:

'It removeth lassitude, vanquisheth heavy dreams, easeth the frame and strengtheneth the memory. It overcometh superfluous sleep and prevents sleepiness in general, so that without trouble whole nights may be spent in study. It is of great avail to men of corpulent bodies and to such as eat much flesh. It clears a dull head and maketh the frame active and hearty.'

The emphasis of the age, nevertheless, was on wine. Taken by themselves, even in the considerable quantities they often were, wine, ale and beer were comparatively harmless, even healthful. However, brandy imported from France was cheap and increasingly popular since the tax on ale and beer had raised their price. Soon the steadily increasing amount of spirits consumed had begun to affect not only the nation's drinking habits, but also the economy. Owing to the decrease in demand for ale and beer the farmers found themselves unable to sell their barley.

As early as 1673 a petition was presented to Parliament with a view to banning the import of brandy, rum, tea and coffee, which read in part:

'Before Brandy, which has now become common and is sold in every little alehouse, came to England in such quantities as it now doth, we drank good strong beer and ale, and all laborious people (which are far the greater part of the kingdom) their bodies requiring after hard labour some strong drink to refresh them, did therefore every morning and evening used to drink a pot of ale or a flagon of strong beer, which greatly helped the promotion of our own grains and did them no great prejudice; it hindereth not their work, nor did it take away their senses, nor cost them much money . . .'

Apart from its own insidious attraction, the reason for the increased brandy drinking was due at least in part to the tax on beer and ale which had not only been retained by successive governments, but had been raised from the original two shillings a barrel to as high as 3s 3d in 1689. On the outbreak of war with France in that year it jumped astronomically to 6s 6d in 1690. In the same year, in a misguided attempt to protect the English corn growers, an Act was passed granting any Englishman the right to distil spirits from home-grown corn. The Act began as follows:

'An Act for the encouraging of the distillation of Brandy and spirits from corn. First, the trade and commerce of France being prohibited, and all their goods from being imported in this kingdom; And whereas good and wholesome Brandy, *aqua vitae* and spirits may be made and drawn from corn; for the encouragement therefore of the making of Brandy, strong waters and spirits from malted corn, and for the greater consumption of corn and the advantage of tillage in this kingdom, the King, Queen and Parliament then assembled have thus ordained it . . .'

One of the immediate side-effects of this policy was to encourage the smugglers, or 'free-traders' as they preferred to be termed, to do their best to ensure that not only brandy, but wine, silks and the latest Paris fashions continued to arrive in spite of the war with France. The inherent dangers of the policy cannot have been apparent at the time, since after four uneasy years of peace and a further outbreak of war, one of the first Acts of Queen Anne's reign was: 'An Act for encouraging the consumption of malted corn for the better preventing the running of French and Foreign Brandy.'

Worse still, the government went on to withdraw the privileges of the Distillers Company, which at least had ensured some control over the distilleries and had prevented the worst sort of spirits being distilled. With this safeguard withdrawn there was no control whatsoever over the distillation of spirits. The effect was disastrous and gave rise to the shameful cheap gin era. This was the period when the five stages of drunkenness were recognised as 'Jocose, Morose, Bellicose, Lachrymose and Comatose'. It gave rise to such wise saws as 'Drink is a good servant, but a bad master'. It also gave rise, in the end, to a national temperance movement, although, like the taste for a new drink, this took the best part of a hundred years before it achieved recognition.

The figures for the annual consumption of distilled spirits in England over this period speak for themselves. In 1694, with a population of six million, they were between 750–800,000 gallons. By 1734, with a population of only six and a quarter million, they had risen to over six million gallons. During this deplorable period, which extended to 1750, they rose to over eight million gallons and since this figure does not take into account illegally distilled spirits or amounts smuggled into the country, the real figure could be anyone's guess, although clearly very much greater. Hogarth's picture of Gin Lane is well known, so, too, is Smollett's description of the scene, written about 1760, but it bears repetition:

'Such a shameful degree of profligacy prevailed that the retailers of this poisonous compound set up printed boards in public inviting people to be drunk for the small expense of one penny, assuring them that they might be dead drunk for twopence and have straw for nothing. They accordingly provided cellars and places strewed with straw, to which they conveyed the wretches who were overwhelmed with intoxication. In these dismal caverns they lay until they recovered some use of their faculties and then they had recourse to the same mischievous compound.'

It is significant that Stow's *Survey of London* of 1720 states:

'The modern sports of the citizens besides drinking are cock-fighting, bowling upon greens, playing at tables, or backgammon, cards, dice and billiards; also musical entertainments, dancing, masks, balls, stage-plays and club meetings in the evening; they sometimes ride out on horse-back and hunt with the lord mayor's pack of dogs when the common hunt goes out. The lower classes divert themselves at football, wrestling, cudgels, nine-pins, shovel-board, cricket, stowball, ringing of bells, quoits, pitching the bar, bear- and bull-baitings, throwing at cocks and lying at alehouses.'

Between 1720 and 1750 there is no doubt that cheap gin had a disastrous effect in London, although outside the metropolis it is doubtful if it had the same impact. The difference between London and the rest of the country was marked. The deaths in London between 1740 and 1742 were double the births, but the death-rate for the whole of the country, as distinct from London, actually fell between 1730 and 1750 when the annual consumption was at its height.

Legislative action was slow, fumbling and ineffectual. In 1729 new duties imposed on manufacturers and retailers were widely evaded. In 1736 the notorious 'Gin Act' imposed a deliberately prohibitive duty of twenty shillings a gallon and a licence fee of £50. This too was virtually ignored and merely had the effect of driving both distillers and retailers underground. Fortunately, subsequent Acts giving the justices greater powers in the matter of granting licences, began to have effect from 1750 onwards and the total consumption of spirits dropped radically, although not before time. By 1758 the consumption of spirits was down to under two million gallons annually.

Another important and far-reaching effect of the policy initiated by William III and of the frequent wars with France during the 18th century was that French wine became harder and harder to obtain. At times it was only due to the activities of the 'Free-traders' that it was obtainable at all and then it was frequently diluted or adulterated in various ways to make it last longer. The really unscrupulous vintners did not hesitate to manufacture their own substitutes. According to Addison, writing in 1709:

'There is in this city a certain fraternity of chymical operators who work underground in holes, caverns and dark retirements, to conceal their mysteries from the eyes and observations of mankind. These subterranean philosophers are daily employed in the transmigration of liquors, and by the power of magical drugs and incantations raise under the streets of London the choicest products of the hills and valleys of France. They can squeeze Bordeaux out of a sloe, and draw Champagne from an apple.'

While travelling in the West Country between Honiton and Exeter during his *Tour of England and Wales* in 1725, Daniel Defoe noted disapprovingly:

'They tell me they send 50,000 hogsheads of cyder hence every year to London, and which is still worse, that it is most of it bought there by the merchants to mix with their wines, which if true, is not much to the reputation of the London vintners.'

Due to such practices and to the overall shortage of French wine, or the high duty on it when obtainable, the taste for it steadily declined in the first half of the 18th century. The confirmed wine drinker turned instead towards the thicker wine obtained duty free under the trade agreement with Portugal. Port indeed became the favourite after-dinner wine in England as a result, although at this time more like a burgundy in character. It was not until 1775 that the first vintage port was produced. Meanwhile, except for those who had travelled abroad and acquired a taste for it, the demand for French wine gradually lapsed entirely. Port and sherry, spirits and beer became the principal drinks of the country.

Between 1710 and 1750 by contrast with the fluctuations of duty on spirits, the duty on beer remained constant at five shillings a barrel. During this period the brewers were forced to compete with the attractions of cheap spirits and in order to gain custom they had to improve their beers and make them more attractive. For the first time they began to concentrate on producing different tasting beers and at the same time altered their appearance and strength.

Three distinct types of beer were evolved, a cheap, dark beer, a more expensive, stronger, more bitter beer containing a greater quantity of hops and finally a light coloured beer, called pale ale, which was produced from the best available barley malt lightly cured in the malt-house. This was the most expensive. Almost inevitably the three beers were frequently demanded mixed together and the resulting drink became known as the 'three threads'.

In addition to these, an extremely dark, heavily hopped, bitter-tasting beer with a very high alcoholic content compared with the other beers was produced, which became a favourite with the porters in the London markets. From this it derived its popular name of 'porter'. This was to remain the most popular beer with many classes of worker until nearly the end of the century. Nor was it only popular in London for it was both brewed and approved as far afield as Glasgow and since it lent itself to production in bulk it resulted in something of a revolution in brewing techniques.

Strong English ale did not meet with universal approval. The anglophile German Pastor, Carl Moritz, journeying in this country in 1782, unexpectedly found himself involved in an all-night drinking session with some Oxford dons. He recorded:

'My health was again *encored*, and drank in strong ale, which, as my company seemed to like it so much, I was sorry I could not like. It either intoxicated or stupefied me; and I do not think it overpowers one much sooner than so much wine would . . . I am almost ashamed to own that, next morning, when I awoke, I had got so dreadful an headach, from the numerous and copious toasts of my jolly and reverend friends, that I could not possibly get up . . .'

In Windsor he found one thing very much the same as in his country:

'Directly under my room was the tap-room; from which I could plainly hear too much of the conversation of some low people, who were drinking and singing songs, in which, as far as I could understand them, there were as many passages at least as vulgar and nonsensical as ours.'

Another foreigner, a Frenchman, François de la Rochefoucauld, visiting the country in 1784, was surprised to find that cock-fighting was a popular sport. He described the scene with some distaste:

'It is conducted in this way: they have a large round table covered with a carpet, and two cocks, of a particular breed, with a lust for battle, are set upon it. Their wings and tails are clipped; their beaks are filed down a little and to each of their legs a strong steel spur is firmly fixed. This is the weapon with which they fight. The spectators make enormous bets and have the keenest interest in the cock on which they have put their money. After they have fought a number of rounds and have freely used their spurs, it nearly always happens that both cocks are almost equally exhausted and both covered with blood. At length one of them, with a supreme effort, overpowers and kills his adversary. The whole fight sometimes lasts three or four hours. All fighting cocks have names which are known throughout the country; their breeds are most carefully preserved and they are fed and trained with a view to getting them into as vigorous a condition as possible. They fight with incredible ferocity and never flag until one of them is killed. Sometimes the victor dies soon after his defeated rival . . . It is a cruel sport, a relic of barbarism, which one cannot forgive in a nation like the English.'

From a sporting viewpoint it was an age of gambling and dicing, horse-racing and hunting, above all fox-hunting, of pugilism and cock-fighting. These were the sports of the Squire and the Corinthian. Bowls, quoits, skittles, fives, football and cricket were all popular games out of doors, the outdoor sports of the inn and the alehouse. Cards, shovel-board (the forerunner of shove-halfpenny) and billiards had begun to take their place in the inn and the alehouse also. The cruder sports of the Middle

Drinkers in a tavern: 1773

Distillery : 1839

Ages and the Elizabethans, throwing at cocks, bull- and badger-baiting were becoming less common, although still practised in some districts.

The Squire and the Parson were the principal figures around which the village life still centred, but, though the Church remained the spiritual centre of village life, increasingly the inn was becoming the temporal centre. Here it was that much of the village life centred. With the growing popularity of cricket it might be that the village blacksmith or the Squire's gardener was the acting captain of the village cricket team and both he and the Squire would happily play together on the green intent on beating the visiting team from a neighbouring village. Or the Squire and his friends might join in a cock-fight in the village inn along with the villagers. The ready sharing of such sporting enjoyments by all classes was an important factor in preventing England from lapsing into revolution as happened in so many cases on the Continent.

As well as giving his impressions of cock-fighting, François de la Rochefoucauld also recorded his views on the English drinking habits and their cooks, as follows:

'Throughout the whole of England the drinking of tea is general. You have it twice a day and though the expense is considerable, the humblest peasant has his tea twice a day, just like the rich man; the total consumption is immense. The high cost of sugar, or molasses, of which large quantities are required, does not prevent this custom being a universal one, to which there are no exceptions . . . The popular beverage is beer, of which there are five or six kinds. The best known is "small beer", but even this is dearer than wine in France . . . In some counties cider is drunk, but it is not as common as beer. The wine ordinarily served is port. The English have exclusive trading rights with Portugal on the express condition that they drink her wine. It is so bad and thick that, unless the British took it as part of their trade bargain, the Portuguese would not be able to get rid of it. Bad as it is it costs five francs a bottle. The government has imposed such enormous duties upon French wine that only the very rich can afford it . . . It is retailed at ten or twelve francs a bottle. English cooks are not very clever folk and even in the best houses one fares ill. The height of luxury is to have a Frenchman, but few people can afford this . . .'

Both Moritz and de la Rochefoucauld commented on the speed of the stage-coaches, which then averaged between seven and eight miles an hour. With the improvement in the roads and service in the first three decades of the 19th century they were soon travelling at a steady twelve miles an hour. The sight of them passing at a spanking trot with the harness jingling and the coach horns sounding seems genuinely to have moved the spectators to delight. William Cobbett summed it up thus:

'Next to a fox-hunt the finest sight in England is a stage-coach just ready to start.'

Certainly it always seems to have been guaranteed to attract a crowd of spectators outside the inn. The sight of the horses newly-harnessed and glistening from the stables, champing at their bits while the ostlers held their heads, and the stage-coach driver, the focus of all eyes, clad in his many-caped driving coat, carefully inspecting the turn-out before preparing to mount the box, with his outside passengers, and the guard behind ready with his 'yard of tin', must have been exciting. Quite aside from all this, there was the bustle of serving wenches, boots, stable lads and other helping hands assisting late travellers on board, with perhaps the added presence of the innkeeper himself standing in the doorway of his inn surveying the well-balanced loaded coach. The scene has been portrayed many times, but even at second-hand it does not fail to stir the imagination. There is always a certain glamour in the air at any departure point, whether railway station, quayside, or airport, but this must have been exceptional and it is clear that it impressed itself on the minds and memories of all who saw it. But by 1825 the Stockton to Darlington railway had opened and change was in the air. Within another twenty years the coaches would no longer be economic.

Meanwhile, true to the tradition that no new drink escaped criticism and opposition, even tea had suffered from its critics. Among these was Jonas Hanway, the eccentric philanthropist, who pioneered the use of the umbrella. In 1757 he complained:

'Will the sons and daughters of this happy isle for ever submit to the bondage of so tyrannical a custom as drinking tea? . . . It is an epidemic disease . . . You see labourers who are mending the road drinking their tea . . . Were they the sons of tea-sippers who won the fields of Crecy and Agincourt, or dyed the Danube's shores with Gallic blood?'

Even as late as 1821 William Cobbett, writing in his *Cottage Economy*, stated roundly:

'I view the tea drinking as a destroyer of health, an enfeebler of the frame, an engenderer of effeminacy and laziness, a debaucher of youth and a maker of misery for old age.'

Of course, Cobbett supported the home brewing of beer, which by this time had become uneconomic, and he noted:

'... to show Englishmen forty years ago that it was good for them to brew beer in their houses would have been as impertinent as gravely to insist that they ought to endeavour not to lose their breath for in those times to have a house and not to brew was a rare thing indeed. Mr. Ellman, an old man and a large farmer in Sussex has recently given in evidence before a Committee of the House of Commons this fact that forty years ago there was not a labourer in his parish that did not brew his own beer and that now there is not one that does it, except by chance the malt be given him.'

The reason for this was simple enough, although a warning against attempting to put economic theories into practice. In his *Wealth of Nations*, the first of all books on the theory of economics, Adam Smith had condemned the beer duty as only affecting beer for sale. A firm believer in his theories was Lord North, prime minister during the American War of Independence, who accordingly raised a direct tax on malt in 1780, so that the private brewer was taxed at the same rate as the brewer producing a thousand barrels. Not unnaturally, one result was that the private brewers quickly found it uneconomic to brew their own beer. Another was that the brewers profited greatly, adding increasingly to their 'tied' retail outlets in the process.

A matter of fifty years too late, in 1830, Parliament tried to remedy the situation by, as they fondly hoped, removing the stranglehold of the brewers and reducing the price of beer to the working man. The Sale of Beer Act, which became popularly known as the Duke of Wellington's Act, since he was prime minister at the time, abolished the duty on beer and allowed anyone to open a beer shop for the sale of beer on the payment of two guineas. Like much legislation on drink it was to have very different effects to that intended.

The immediate result was a vast proliferation of beer shops all over the country. In the first year there were 24,000 and by 1836 46,000. Unfortunately few of them brewed their own beer. Almost all of them, or certainly the vast majority, found it more convenient to obtain their beer direct from the breweries. Although it may have been cheaper, the general standard of beer served was a good deal lower in such establishments.

Nor was the sale of gin and other spirits greatly reduced as had been hoped. Once again the brewers profited greatly.

By 1844 the railways had virtually ended the coaching era, although some coach services carried on to the end of the 19th century in Scotland and the West Country. By the middle of the century the snorting locomotives had taken over all the traffic and the coaching inns were left without any trade worth mentioning. The roads were deserted save for farmers' waggons, private coaches and gigs. Even if it had benefited by the service provided by the railways, the countryside had lost something in the process.

If the Georgian age had tended towards change and experimentation, the Victorian era tended towards legislation and consolidation. It was the age of the social reformers and temperance enthusiasm. Although two previous bills to declare bull-baiting illegal, in 1802 and 1829, had both been defeated, it was finally declared illegal in 1835. In 1849 cock-fighting, too, was prohibited by law. Although the former had to all intents and purposes lapsed, cock-fighting was still carried on secretly by scattered groups of enthusiastic devotees until the turn of the century.

Before 1900 one further drink began to be popular in England. Throughout the 18th century illicit whisky stills had flourished in Scotland, particularly in the Highlands, where everyone regarded it as their native right to distil 'Usquebaugh'. The situation had only finally been brought under control, or something approaching control, in the second quarter of the 19th century. At that time, however, there was little sale for the Highland malt whiskies or the Lowland grain whiskies, neither of which were very palatable to the English taste. Even when the two were successfully blended in the 1860s to make the first blended Scotch whiskies, it was found that the upper class Englishmen were too addicted to brandy to change. In the 1880s, however, the vineyards of the Grande Champagne in the centre of the Cognac area were devastated by the deadly *Phylloxera vastatrix*, an insect which destroys the roots of the vine. By the 1890s there were no stocks of cognac left and the English turned enthusiastically to whisky instead.

By the turn of the century another potential herald of change had appeared. The first motor-cars were to be seen on the roads. It only remained for the Wright brothers to make their epic flight in 1908 and the 20th century was truly under way. Yet at the time, the speed of the changes to come was far from apparent. The Edwardian era was one of glitter and gaiety, of champagne and 'blue ruin', of free spending and squalor, of gaslight and explosive politics. Yet income tax was negligible, beer and porter were cheap, cigarettes, tobacco and spirits were barely taxed at all, shove-halfpenny, cards, darts, dominoes and similar games could be played in any public house. The village inn was still the centre of village life and cricket was still played on the village green. With the outbreak of the 1914 War nothing was ever to be quite the same again, but meanwhile, to the man in the bar, the biggest danger seemed to be the demands of the temperance movement for early closing hours. Britain had never seemed more solidly set in her ways.

Chapter Three

Alehouses, Inns and Taverns

Origins with Romans – Anglo-Saxon Inns – King Edgar's Decree on Inns – Distinction between Alehouse, Inn and Tavern – Role of Church in Mediaeval World – Piers Plowman – Canterbury Tales – Effects of Dissolution of Monasteries – 1552 Licensing Act – Tippling Houses – William Harrison on Inns – Fynes Morison on Inns – John Taylor in Somerset – Survey of Twenty-Six Counties – Effects of Civil War

In Southwark at the Tabbard as I lay . . .
At night was come into that hostlerie
Wel nyne and twentye in a companye . . .
That toward Canterbury wolden ryde.
The chambres and the stables weren wyde,
And wel we weren lodged at the beste.

The Prologue: The Canterbury Tales: GEOFFREY CHAUCER: *c.* 1388.

THE EXACT ORIGINS of alehouses, inns and taverns are obscure, but it seems most likely that in the hundred years following Julius Caesar's invasion of Britain in 55 B.C. the Romans introduced them to this country, together with their excellent road system. Ale was already well known and, no doubt, in the towns they built, the Romans added such refinements as shops, or alehouses, dispensing ale and even possibly wine. They understood the need for rest houses for travellers and in conjunction with their roads they almost inevitably introduced some type of inn or tavern. Just what form these took is now uncertain, but it is reasonable to assume that along with other such civilised practices as baths, we owe to the Romans the origins of the English Inn.

It is known that the Anglo-Saxons had alehouses and taverns since there are various references to them amongst their laws and enactments. One of the earliest of these is a canon promulgated in the 8th century by the then Archbishop of York, which decreed that: 'No priest go to eat or drink in a tavern'. Later on, King Edgar, whose reign extended from 957–975, laid down that there were too many alehouses and that their numbers should be restricted to one only in each village. From these and other fragments it is possible to gather some idea of the overall picture.

The alehouse, it is clear, provided ale and some degree of entertainment for the customer. The tavern appears to have been rather more substantial providing wine as well as food and entertainment and possibly also some primitive lodging for travellers. The inn, however, was primarily intended to provide food and lodging for travellers, as well as providing them with ale and entertainment. The principal difference was that the tavern provided wine and theoretically no lodging, whereas the inn provided lodging and theoretically no wine. In many cases, however, the distinction between inn and tavern seems to have been blurred and in some instances the alehouse seems to have usurped the functions of both. Inevitably, over the centuries, in various parts of the country, there must have been many times when the dividing line between them was anything but clear-cut.

In the mediaeval world the alehouse was the commonest institution of the three, for then hospitality was still regarded as a duty. The traveller would be entertained, according to his rank, in castle, manor house or ecclesiastical foundation. The hazards of travelling, the extreme badness of the roads, decayed beyond recognition from the days of the Romans, the dangers from footpads or roving bands of outlaws, and the need for guides in many areas, ensured that no-one travelled unless from sheer necessity.

The enormously important role of the Church in the mediaeval world must also be taken into account. With the introduction of shrines containing holy relics the devout began to make annual pilgrimages, and to provide them with food and lodging the Church established hospices, often of considerable size, such as that at Maidstone in Kent built by Bishop Boniface. These hostels were often established adjacent to the abbey or monastery which founded them and there the pilgrims were entitled to two days' rest and lodging according to their rank, being expected to contribute as they felt they might.

The nobler and wealthier visitor could expect fine wines from France and venison from the abbot's park or carp from his fishponds. His accommodation would be of a similar high standard. For the less wealthy there would still be ale brewed by the monks themselves, which was regarded as the finest in Europe, and reasonable victuals and lodging. With such accommodation available there was little need for inns or taverns, although the latter certainly existed in the towns for the benefit of the townspeople and the former were sometimes encouraged to take the overflow at some particularly popular centre for pilgrimages, where people might wish to stay for longer than just a few days.

Among the largest source of travellers other than pilgrims and wool merchants were the clerics themselves. Nor were they always particular about ecclesiastical discipline. Archbishop Richard, Thomas à Beckett's successor at Canterbury, was forced to decree in 1175: 'Let no clerks in Holy Orders go to eat in taverns, nor be present at drinking bouts, unless in their travels. Let the offender desist or be deposed.'

As this decree indicates, the alehouses and taverns were often the scenes of considerable debauchery. The poem *Piers Plowman* attributed to William Langland (*c.* 1362) gives a very good description of the scene in an alehouse. The subject of this contemporary satire, Glutton, is met on his way to church by Betty the brewster and invited to try the new brew of ale in her alehouse, where he is greeted with cries of welcome. By that evening he has consumed over a gallon of the ale and has to be supported home to bed by his wife and serving wench. Throughout Saturday and Sunday he sleeps in drunken slumber to awaken on Sunday evening, when his first words are to call afresh for the drinking cup.

The various people to be found in the alehouse are shown to be a very wide cross section of the community. They include a shoemaker, a gamekeeper and his wife, both already drunk when Glutton arrives, a tinker and his apprentices, a parson and a parish clerk, ditchers and harlots, porters and pickpockets, the hangman at Tyburn and many others. Most of them appear to end up the worse for drink and clearly the scene was not an uncommon one, typical also probably of a scot ale, church ale or any similar feast.

Although William Langland's setting was an alehouse, it is unlikely that the company to be found in taverns and inns was much more restrained at times. They, too, catered for a wide cross-section of the community, as Chaucer indicates in the Canterbury Tales. In general, however, the inns at least catered for the rather richer classes who could afford to travel and make a pilgrimage, banding together for their own protection and amusement on the way. In their journeys at the comfortable, lolloping pace which became known as the Canterbury Gallop, or canter, they may have whiled away the time by story-telling or conversation. At their evening halts, whether at a hostel or an inn, as standards rose they expected increasingly to be well boarded and lodged.

As the Prologue to the Canterbury Tales shows, there were already, a hundred years before the Dissolution of the Monasteries in 1539 abruptly curbed the power of the Church, a number of inns such as the Tabard at Southwark, which catered for travellers, wealthy wool merchants and others, but principally pilgrims. Already the number of travellers had increased far beyond the power of chance hospitality or of the ecclesiastical hostels to cope with them alone. With the abrupt termination of the Church's influence, following Henry VIII's drastic action, many of the old hostels were purchased and in lay hands transformed into inns. In the West Country, Somersetshire, Gloucestershire, Oxfordshire, Hampshire and Kent there are still surviving examples of this type of inn which originated as an ecclesiastical hostel.

Already, as early as 1495, an Act had been passed empowering any two Justices of the Peace 'to reject and put away Common ale-selling in towns . . . and to take sureties of keepers of alehouses in their good behaviour'. This was to be followed in 1552 by an Act whereby Justices were given the power both to license and suppress alehouses. These two acts were the forerunners of much further and often complex legislation, but the latter was the cornerstone of the licensing laws and remains the basis of them still today.

During the period of trade expansion in the more settled times of the Tudors, there was inevitably a considerable increase in the number of inns, taverns and alehouses. By 1553 there was felt the need for an Act limiting the number of taverns in the major towns and by this means the amount of wine sold. London had forty, York nine, Bristol six, Cambridge, Canterbury, Chester, Exeter, Gloucester, Hull, Newcastle-on-Tyne and Norwich four, Colchester, Hereford, Ipswich, Lincoln, Oxford, Salisbury, Shrewsbury, Southampton, Westminster, Winchester and Worcester three. By 1577 the numbers had already increased and an incomplete census of that year showed that there were 14,202 alehouses, 1,631 inns and 329 taverns in England and Wales.

One estimate of the total number of inns, taverns and alehouses at that time is in the region of 20,000. With a population of close on three and three-quarter millions this would work out at around one such establishment for rather less than two hundred people throughout the country, compared with the present-day figure of one for every four hundred. At that time, however, tea and coffee were unknown and all ale, or beer, was brewed by the alehouse keepers themselves. The total consumption per head was probably as high as two quarts per day, so that this figure is not unreasonable in the circumstances.

The overall standard of the inns at least seems to have been high. William Harrison in his very evocative *Description of England* written in 1563, recorded:

'Those towns that we call thorowfaires (i.e. on the main roads) have great and sumptuous innes builded in them for the receiving of such travellers and strangers as passe to and fro. The manner of harbouring wherein is not like that of some other countries, in which the host or goodman of the house doth chalenge a lordlie authoritie over his ghests, but clean otherwise. Everie man may use his inne as his own house in England and have for his monie how great or how little varietie of vittels and what other service himself shall think expedient to call for . . . If his chamber be once appointed he may carrie the kei with him as of his own house so long as he lodgeth there. If he lose ought whilst he abideth in the inne, the host is bound by generall custom to restore the damage, so that there is no greater securitie aniewhere for travellers than in the greatest inns of England.'

Writing of his journeys in various countries from 1605 to 1617, Fynes Moryson in his *Itineraries* published some fifty or more years later, echoed the same sentiments regarding English inns. He wrote:

'I have heard some Germans complain of the English Innes by the highway, as well as for deernesse as for that they had only roasted meates . . . But if these strangers had knowne the English tongue . . . surely they should have found thatt the World affords not such Inns as England hath either for good and cheape entertainment after the Guest's pleasure or for humble attendance on passengers, yea even in very poor Villages . . . where should (he) see the thatched houses he would fall into a fainting of his spirits, but if he should smell the variety of meates, his starving looks would be much cheared . . . There is no place in the world where passengers may so freely command as the English Inns and are attended for themselves and their horses as well as if they were at home and perhaps better . . .'

Against these two somewhat eulogistic accounts it is only fair to set an

Act of 1604 designed to increase control over alehouses, which indicates that in these establishments at least all was not so well ordered. It read:

'Whereas the ancient true and principal use of wine, alehouses and victualling houses was for the receipt, relief and lodging of wayfaring people travelling from place to place and . . . not meant for the entertainment or harbouring of lewd idle people to spend and consume their money and time in lewd and drunken manner; it is enacted that only travellers and traveller's friends and labourers for one hour at dinner time, or lodgers, can reccive entertainment under penalty.'

It is notable that many alehouses had begun to obtain their ale or beer from a separate brewer, rather than brew their own. Such establishments were known as 'tippling houses' and were sometimes owned by the brewer with a manager set in charge of them. Throughout the ensuing centuries the continued proliferation of such tippling houses was to remain a problem for successive governments.

For a description of a thoroughly bad inn of the period not much better than an alehouse or tippling house it is necessary to turn to John Taylor (1580–1653), already quoted in defence of ale and condemnation of beer. His literary output of amusing and scurrilous writing was considerable. He made a series of journeys around the country and afterwards wrote about them in both prose and verse. His account of his visit to the Rose and Crown in Nether Stowey under the Quantocks in Somerset, 'a ragged market town' as he described it, seems even by his standards to have been quite exceptional:

'Mine host was very sufficiently drunk, the house most delicately decked with artificial and natural sluttery . . . The walls and ceilings were adorned with rare spiders' tapestry or cobweb-lawn, the smoke was so palpable and perspicuous that I could scarcely see anything else . . . the odours and contagious perfume of that house was able to outflight all the milliners in Christendom . . . To comfort me completely mine host swigged off half a pot to me, bade me be merry and asked me if I would have any powdered beef and carrots for supper. I told him yea with all my heart . . . and sat three hours . . . At last seven of the clock was struck . . . the fire was out, no beef to be boiled, mine host fast asleep, the maid tending the hogs and my hungry self half-starved with expectation. I awakened mine host and asked him where the beef was; he told me he had none and desired me to be contented with eggs fried with parsley. I bade him show me to my chamber, which he did; the chamber was suitable to the rest of the house. There I stayed till near nine o'clock expecting fried eggs, when mine host came to me with an empty answer; there were no eggs to be had, so at the last I purchased a piece of bread and butter and to bed and then began my further torments, for thinking to take a little rest, I was furiously assaulted by an Ethiopian army of fleas, and it may be freely believed that I laid so manfully about me that I made more than five hundred *mortuus est*. They were so well grown that as I grabbed them I gave 'em no quarter, but rubbed 'em between my fingers and thumb like new boiled peas . . . At last weariness and watching began to force sleep upon me, so that in spite of the fleas' teeth I began to wink, when suddenly three children began to cry, and for an hour's space I was kept waking, which made me fall to the slaughter again. The children being hushed asleep, the game began from among the dogs, for the cry was up, and the bawling curs took the air one from the other all the town over, and the dogs no sooner done than the day break appeared and the hogs began to cry out for their breakfast, so I arose and travelled, almost sleeping, towards Dunster.

From nasty rooms, that never felt brooms,
From excrements and all bad scents,
From children's bawling and caterwauling,
From grunting of hogs and barking of dogs,
And from biting of fleas I found my ease.'

It is only fair to add that three military gentlemen from the 'Military Company in Norwich', a Captain, a Lieutenant and an Ensign, who made a *Tour of Twenty-six Counties in Seven Weeks* in 1634 found themselves extraordinarily well looked after wherever they stayed. The inns in general at this period prior to the Civil War seem to have attained a very high standard throughout the country. The worst that the three officers could find to complain about was a landlord in Lancaster whom they found a 'surley and touchy Lad', but even he had his good points and proved a useful informant about the district. Their only other complaint in one or two places was the amount they were charged, but even then they were prepared to admit they had received good value and in several instances they considered their charges extremely moderate.

The Civil War and period of the Commonwealth rule must have been an extremely difficult time for the keepers of alehouses, inns and taverns especially. Almost inevitably the sympathies of most of them were with the Royalists although the majority were inhibited by their trade from taking sides too openly. Even if their loyalties lay with the Parliamentary cause they were the natural target for attacks by the Puritans with their bigotted narrowness of mind and outlook. To be connected with the brewing or selling of intoxicating liquor was enough to put them beyond the pale at once. As for encouraging frivolous games on their premises, this was naturally anathema to the militant religious bigots.

An example of what the innkeepers had to put up with at this time is contained in an order of 1656 to the Justice of Hertfordshire:

'Forasmuch as His Highness the Lord Protector of the Commonwealth hath taken special note of the mischiefs and great disorders which daily happen and are committed in Taverns, Inns and Alehouses . . . The Justices of this County of Hertford are adjoined to take special care for the suppressing of all such alehouse keepers as are, or shall be, convicted of the prophanation of the Lord's Day by receiving into their houses any company, or of swearing, drunkenness, suffering tippling, gaming, or playing at Tables, Billiard Table, Shovel Board, Cards, Dice, Ninepins, Pigeon-Holes, Trunks, or of keeping a Bowling Green or Bowling Alley or any of them or any other games.'

In the face of such stringent regulations it is surprising that any alehouses, inns or taverns survived, even if the justices were themselves Royalists and not disposed to enforce such regulations too strictly. Yet survive they did and no doubt the Landlords greeted the Restoration with even more relief than their most loyal customers. Whether the standard of the inns was quite the same is another matter. Whether it was merely that after the Civil War the number of travellers on the roads steadily increased, with more opportunities for poor inns to be noted, it is hard to say. It can only be noted that whereas before the Civil War bad inns were apparently extremely rare, thereafter they became gradually more common. It is difficult, however, to lay the blame for that on the Puritan regime. It is probably true to say that each age gets the inns it deserves.

Chapter Four

From Alehouse to Gin Palace

Pepys on Alehouses and Taverns – Outside London – Defoe on Coffee Houses – Development of the Coffee House – Addison's Sir Roger de Coverley in one – Dr. Johnson on Taverns – Pastor Moritz on Inns – At Nettlebed – Near Nottingham – de la Rochefoucauld – Byng – Hints on Inns – At Newnham – Winchester – Rugby – Middleham – Wansford – Samuel Bamford, hints for foot travellers in an Inn – Gin Palaces – The Railway Age – M. Esquiros

Who'er has travelled life's dull round,
Where'er his stages may have been,
May sigh to think he still has found
The warmest welcome – at an Inn.

WILLIAM SHENSTONE: 1714–1763.

ONE OF THE principal sources of information about the eating and drinking habits of the 17th century, about the customs of London in particular, is, of course, the diarist Samuel Pepys. His constant references to alehouses, taverns, coffee houses and inns shed a light on the way of life of the day which no other source can equal. Three of his entries concerning alehouses and taverns in London will suffice to indicate the scope of their entertainment and hospitality:

'9th February 1660 . . . Thence, Swan and I to a drinking house near Temple-Bar; where while he writ, I played of my flagelette till a dish of poached eggs was got ready for us; which we eat and so by coach home.'

'6th March 1660 . . . So I went to the Bell, where was Mr.'s Eglin, Veezy, Vincent a butcher, one more and Mr. Tanner, with whom I played upon a viall and he the vialin after dinner, and were very merry, with a special good dinner – a leg of veal and bacon, two capons and sausages and fritters, with abundance of wine. After that I went home . . .'

'6th November 1661. Going forth this morning, I met Mr. Davenport and a friend of his, one Mr. Furbisher, to drink their morning draught with me; and I did give it to them in good wine and anchoves, and pickled oysters; and took them to the Sun in fish streete and there did give them a barrel of good ones and a great deal of wine, and sent for Mr. W. Bernard (Sir Robts. son, a grocer hereabouts) and were very merry; and cost me a good deal of money; And at noon left them, with my head full of wine . . .'

Outside London the standard of the taverns and inns was not so high. From Pepys' diaries we find that travel by coach was slow and expensive still and that guides were required to ensure that the traveller did not lose his way. Even this does not always seem to have saved them from getting lost. On a journey to Bristol in June 1668 he recorded:

'10th (Wednesday) Come to the George Inn (Salisbury) where lay in a silk bed and very good diet. To supper and then to bed.

'11th (Thursday) . . . paid the reckoning, (£2. 5s 6d) which was so exorbitant and particular in rate of my horses and 7s 6d for bread and beer that I was mad . . . Thence about six o'clock and with a guide went over the smooth Plain . . . with great difficulty come about ten o'clock to a little inn, where we were fain to go into a room where a pedlar was in bed, and made him rise; and there my wife and I lay, and in a truckle bed, Betty Turner and Willett, but good beds and the master of the house a sober, understanding man, and I had a great discourse with him about this country's matters, as wool and corne and other things. And he also merry and made us mighty merry at supper . . . By and by to bed, glad of this mistake because it seems had we gone on as we intended we could not have passed with our coach and must have lain on the Plain all night . . .

'12th (Friday) Up, finding our beds good, but lousy; which made us merry, the reckoning and servants coming to 9s 6d; my guide thither 2s . . .'

There was a slow but steady improvement both in the means of travel on the roads and in the roads themselves, as well as in the standards of inns during the fifty or so years between the end of Pepys's Diaries and the comprehensive *Tour of England and Wales* undertaken by Daniel Defoe in 1725. He noted considerable improvements taking place in the roads and commented on it at intervals. He also approved the standards of the inns in several widely separated areas, but his tour was rather an overall appraisal of the country than an individual traveller's views on travel in the country. In Shrewsbury, however, he recorded that there were 'the most coffee houses . . . that ever I saw in any town, but when you come into them they are but alehouses, only they think that the name of coffee house gives them a better air.'

The latter part of the 17th century and the early part of the 18th century saw the rapid growth in popularity of the coffee house as a meeting place. People who had previously dropped in at a tavern for their morning draught of wine, taking a room to write a letter, discuss the latest news or do business with friends, or even play the flageolette as Pepys had done, turned increasingly to the coffee house instead. One of the reasons for this was the increasing shortage of good wine from 1690 onwards. Another was the convenience and comparative cheapness of it. To drop in at a coffee house, take a dish of tea or coffee and glance at the daily papers involved at the most a gossip with a friend about the latest news. It did not involve the danger of innumerable toasts and the possibility of a thick head all afternoon. Very soon the verb to 'coffee house' was coined as meaning to indulge in conversation and in the City of London the coffee houses were recognised centres for the exchange of business and information. It was from Lloyds coffee house where the ships' captains and insurance agents met that the present insurance brokers centre, the largest of its kind in the world, was developed.

A good description of the contemporary scene in a coffee house is afforded by Addison's sketch of his famous character Sir Roger de Coverley visiting one:

'He asked me if I would smoke a pipe with him over a cup of coffee at Squire's . . . I accordingly waited on him to the coffee house where his venerable figure drew upon us the eye of the whole room. He had no sooner seated himself at the upper end of the high table but he called for a clean pipe, a paper of tobacco, a dish of coffee, a wax candle and the Supplement with such an air of cheerfulness and good humour that all the boys in the coffee room (who seemed to take pleasure in serving him) were at once employed on his several errands insomuch that nobody else

The George Inn at Glastonbury

The Harmonic Every Evening.

New and Splendid Room.

CYDER CELLARS.

MAIDEN LANE

COVENT GARDEN

JOHN REGAN

Having at an immence expence completed his improvements, trusts his exertions will merit from a discerning Public, a continuance of that support and, general patronage, which this Old Established Place of Resort has for so many years received.

Wines, Chops, Spirits, Dinners, &c. of the best Quality, and Moderate Charges.

Maggs, Printer, Stationer, and Newsman, Knightsbridge.

could come at a dish of tea until the Knight had got all his conveniences about him.'

By the second half of the 18th century no inn of any size was complete without its coffee room, generally placed close to the entrance hall for the convenience of travellers. Although an eminent conversationalist himself, there is little doubt that Dr. Samuel Johnson preferred an inn or a tavern to a coffee house. In one of his pontifications, admiringly recorded by Boswell, he analysed the reasons why it was preferable to stay in a good inn rather than a private house. He argued:

'There is no private house in which people can enjoy themselves as well as at a capital tavern. Let there be ever so great a plenty of good things, ever so much grandeur, ever so much elegance, ever so much desire that everybody should be easy, in the nature of things it cannot be; there must always be some degree of care and anxiety, the master of the house is anxious to entertain his guests; the guests are anxious to be agreeable to him; and no man but a very impudent dog indeed can freely command what is in another man's house as if it were his own. Whereas at a tavern, there is general freedom from anxiety. You are sure you are welcome; and the more noise you make, the more trouble you give, the more things you call for, the welcomer you are. No servants will attend you with the alacrity which waiters do, who are incited by the prospects of an immediate reward in proportion as they please. No, sir, there is nothing which has yet been conceived by man, by which so much happiness is produced as by a good tavern or inn.'

It is very doubtful if Carl Moritz, whose journey in 1782 was on foot, would have agreed with Dr. Johnson's philosophy. He was never sure of his welcome. Of course at that time travelling on foot was regarded as a sign of poverty and not considered respectable. As he himself admitted that he seldom washed his shirts and he does not seem to have been over particular about shaving either, he must have appeared in English eyes an altogether rather eccentric figure. With the additional handicap of a foreign accent he no doubt looked a thoroughly suspicious character and he was turned away from numerous inns where he asked to spend the night, even sometimes having the door slammed in his face. After this had happened to him in Henley he was forced to walk five miles further on to Nettlebed, where his description of the inn and the different treatment he received to that of some travellers who arrived by post-chaise is very revealing:

'I arrived rather late in the evening, when it was indeed quite dark. Everything seemed to be all alive in this little village; there was a party of militia soldiers who were dancing, singing and making merry. Immediately on my entrance into the village, the first house that I saw lying on my left was an inn, from which as usual in England, a large beam extended across the street to the opposite house, from which hung dangling an astonishingly large sign with the name of the proprietor.

'May I stay here tonight?' I asked with eagerness: 'Why, yes you may'; an answer which, however cold and surly, made me exceedingly happy.

'They showed me into the kitchen and set me down to sup at the same table with some soldiers and the servants . . . While I was eating a post-chaise drove up and in a moment both the folding doors were thrown open, and the whole house set in motion in order to receive with all due respect, these guests, who, no doubt were supposed to be persons of consequence. The gentlemen alighted, however, only for a moment and called for nothing but a couple of pots of beer; and then drove away again. Notwithstanding the people of the house behaved to them with all possible attention, for they came in a post-chaise.

'Though this was an ordinary village inn, and they certainly did not take me for a person of consequence, they yet gave me a carpeted bedroom and a very good bed.'

Although Moritz complained bitterly about his treatment as a foot traveller it never occurred to him to blame his own disreputable appearance. The fact that he was received at all and generally quite favourably speaks volumes for the standards of hospitality of those inns which accepted him. Naturally they catered more especially for the coach traveller since to them this generally meant better custom. Yet in spite of his occasional obtuseness Moritz was a keen observer encountering some varied company and some varied inns during his travels. Perhaps amongst his most interesting descriptions was that of a night spent amongst some colliers near Nottingham.

'I at last came to another inn where was written on the sign "The Navigation Inn" because it is the storehouse of the colliers of Trent. A rougher or ruder kind of people I never saw than these colliers, whom I here met assembled in the kitchen, and in whose company I was obliged to spend the evening.

'Their language, their dress, their manners, were, all of them, singularly vulgar and disagreeable; and their expressions still more so; They hardly spoke a word without adding a G. D. me to it, and thus cursing, quarrelling, drinking, singing and fighting, they seemed to be pleased and to enjoy the evening. I must do them the justice to add that none of them however at all molested me, or did me any harm. On the contrary, every one again and again drank my health and I took care not to forget to drink theirs in return . . . as often as I drank, I never omitted to say "Your healths gentlemen all." . . .

'The landlady, who sat in the kitchen along with this goodly company, was nevertheless well dressed, and a remarkably well-looking woman. As soon as I had supped, I hastened to bed, but could not sleep; my quondam companions, the colliers, made such a noise the whole night through – In the morning, when I got up, there was not one to be seen or heard.'

There were, of course, no opening or closing hours in those days and an inn, or an alehouse such as this appears to have been, could stay open as long as its customers required. The fact that the kitchen appears to have been the centre for the entire company is an interesting point. Possibly, if Moritz had arrived in more impressive circumstances, in a post-chaise for instance, he might have been offered a room to himself, but had he been travelling in this way he would probably not have stopped there in the first place.

François de la Rochefoucauld travelling in greater style and comfort two years later in 1784 was very impressed with the standards of the inns he saw and wrote:

'It is a very remarkable thing that at Ipswich, which is a large town and the capital of a large county, there is not a single inn which is even passable; whereas generally you find them in unpretentious villages to be quite excellent and lacking in nothing – not even in cleanliness.'

An experienced traveller of the period between 1780 and the early 1790s was the Hon. John Byng, afterwards briefly 5th Viscount Torrington in succession to his brother from whom he was estranged for most of his life. A soldier for the first part of his life, Byng retired as a Major and took a post in the Inland Revenue Office which seems to have been a dull but reasonably well paid sinecure. He had time enough to make a considerable number of leisurely tours of the country on horseback, generally accompanied by a servant and a dog, but sometimes alone. During these journeys he stayed at inns of all sorts and descriptions and recorded his impressions of them in his diaries. These records provide glimpses of the life of the period and more especially the standards of the inns at a time when those standards were very rapidly changing.

Having been on active service, Byng knew how to take care of himself when necessary on his travels and by bitter experience he acquired a very shrewd idea of what to expect. He was scathing about the monotony of inn meals, referring to the 'eternal boiled chicken', which was one of his pet anathemas. At the start of one of his early journeys to the West Country in 1781 he mentioned a useful method he had discovered of making sure of a good midday meal:

'At Newnham, a small market town . . . I entered the Bear Inn with a good appetite and found a round of beef just taken from the pot; which I strove to devour, likewise a gooseberry pie. It is always my rule to stop (if possible) about noon at second rate inns and take the family fare; as one commonly dines better in that way and at half the expense of an ordered dinner.'

Another thing Byng could not stand was damp sheets and he recorded his views on the subject with his customary forthrightness:

'As for my sheets, I always take them with me, knowing that next to a certainty five sheets must be dirty and three damp out of number ten; these with a very few other necessaries travel behind my servant; as for my nightcap, great coat and such other etceteras they travel behind my own person in a small cloakbag.'

Unfortunately for him, he was travelling without his servant in 1782 when he wrote:

'August 24th . . . Wet and tired I put up at the George Inn at Winchester; where from my portmanteau and want of attendants, no civil treatment cou'd be got, or for some time any room for myself; till at last, by calling about me lustily, I avoided being put in a room with servants; and by dint of perseverance, took care of myself, my horse and my dog . . . Here at last I did procure (another) boiled chicken for my supper and pen and ink for my entertainment, and so betwixt eating, writing, dog and horse, pass'd the time till the hour for retiring arrived.

'August 25th. My bed was equally unpleasant with the rest of my treatment; and adding as little to my composure; sleep was not to be found and thro' the night I sweated on a soft feather bed and dirty blankets, wishing for the morning's light. I then had a long business of dressing, brushing and bracing myself with coffee. I left Winton as soon as possible and an inn, dirty, insolent and ill-conducted.'

Something appears to have gone wrong with his arrangements regarding sheets when he visited Rugby in 1789, but despite this he commented very favourably on the charges:

'My sheets were so damp and the blankets so dirty and stinking, and the room so smelling of putridity that I slept little; tho' I took off the sheets and employed all the brandy, near a pint, in purifying the room and sprinkling the quilt and blankets . . . glad was I to rise, tho' with an head-ach and gloomy as the day . . . This our Rugby charge – *for one night – two meals and 3 horses* (Eating 2s; Tea 1s 4d: Wine 2s: Punch 2s: Horses, Hay and Corn 4s 3d: Total 11s 7d) will prove touring to be no very extravagant pleasure; and silence the ignorant assertions I often hear that all travelling is wonderfully expensive.'

Reactionary as he often was and ready to condemn the faults of many inns, Byng was still willing to acknowledge both good food and good service when he encountered them. When he visited an inn at Middleham in Yorkshire in 1792 he recorded:

'G. led the horses down the hill into the town to what seem'd to be a sorry inn; however it yielded well (for they spake of their trout and of their cold larder with reason) and I was shown into a clean parlour up one pair of stairs. I not only ordered several trout for dinner, but now dictate their cookery and prevent the frying and the parsley and the fennel and the butter and substitute boiling and anchovy sauce; as for cold things they introduce cold ham, cold beef, cold fowl and gooseberry pye . . . The port wine and the ale seemed equally good . . . I now felt a haste for dinner and this is a description of it:

A Boiled Fowl

Cold Ham Yorkshire Pudding Gooseberry Pye

Loyn of Mutton Roast Cheesecakes

A better dinner and better dress'd I never sat down to; but I fear the charge will be *heavy* – 1s 6d at least: . . . White Swan, Middleham: June 9: Dinner 1s 3d: Wine 2s 6d: Supper 1s: Brandy 1s 2d: June 10th: Breakfast 9d; Dinner 1s 3d: Wine 2s 6d: Supper 1s; Wine 1s 3d: June 11th: Breakfast 9d: Horses 3s 4d: Corn 4s: Paper 1d: £1 0s 11d. I was close to my guess at their (unconsciable) charge.'

Byng's habit of including his bills as well as his uninhibited comments provides a very clear picture of the overall standard of the inns and it seems obvious that towards the turn of the century with ever increasing travel on the roads it was improving, although there were also some very bad inns to be found. Byng, himself, was a keen fisherman and play-goer and to some extent this coloured his preferences. Although a keen critic he also had his own favourite inn of which he wrote affectionately as follows:

'I came in quite happy to that excellent house, The Haycock, Wansford Bridge, where I am at home; and Mrs Norton met me with "Pray Sir, walk into your *own* room". All so neat and comfortable with pens, paper and wafers in my *own* room. The waiter said: "Sir, roast beef, potatoes and fresh tarts will be ready at half past one o'clock." I shall often return here, I hope, for where can I find a better inn: see a better bridge; or catch more fish? The mail coach arrives regularly at seven o'clock every morning; northwards; and at five every evening; southwards: Two theatres within five miles; that's extraordinary.'

As Byng's diaries clearly show, by the turn of the century the effects of stage-coach travel were already pronounced and the roads were increasingly filled with traffic. The inns were finding the results profitable and the cleavage between alehouses or tippling houses, and inns was becoming more noticeable than ever. In many cases the alehouses or tippling houses were owned by a brewery, whereas, as yet, the majority of inns of any standing were independent, although more and more were coming to rely on the breweries for their beer.

With the industrial revolution, the population was steadily increasing and, even if they were still not approved by the inns, foot travellers were no longer quite so uncommon. Samuel Bamford, walking from Manchester to London in 1819, afterwards recorded his method of ensuring lodgings each night:

'A foot traveller, if he is really desirous to obtain lodgings, should never stand about asking about them. He should walk into a good room – never into the common tap-room – put his dusty feet under a table, ring the bell pretty smartly, and order something to eat and drink, and not speak in the humblest of tones. He will be served quickly and respectfully – that is, if those two things happen to be understood at the house. After his repast he should take out his pipe or cigar, if he be a smoker, and whether he be or not, he should drink, chat, and make himself quite at ease until bed-time, when all he has to do will be to call the chambermaid and ask her to light him to bed. That will be done as a matter of course, and he will probably have saved himself a tramp round the town in search of lodgings, and, probably, after all, the making of his own bed under a manger or in a hay-loft.'

During the 1830s and early 1840s the coaching era reached its peak and the inns on the coaching routes flourished as never before. In 1830, however, the Sale of Beer Act resulted, as we have seen, in a sudden enormous proliferation of beer shops throughout England. The alehouses or tippling houses suffered an inevitable loss of custom and in an effort to retain their old custom, or to attract new customers, the breweries were forced to rebuild, redecorate and refurnish many of their properties. By this time the tippling house had come to be recognised as a 'public house', and the old alehouse proper was increasingly rare. The report by an eye-witness of how one 'low, dirty, public house with only one doorway' was converted in this manner in London described the result as:

'A handsome edifice, the front ornamented with pilasters supporting a handsome cornice . . . the whole elevation remarkably striking and handsome; the doorways were increased . . . to three, and each of these eight to ten feet wide . . . and the doors and windows glazed with very large single squares of glass, and the gas fittings of the most costly description . . . when the doors were opened the rush was tremendous; it was instantly filled with customers and continued so till midnight.'

It was in such 'Gin Palaces' as they were soon nick-named that the effects of the Industrial Revolution quickly began to be apparent. The foreman preferred not to drink with his men and paid an extra halfpenny for his beer to be separate from them. From this stemmed the saloon and public bar division which has survived to this day. It was such social distinctions which also produced the movable screens or panels of the Victorian days which could be swivelled round to ensure privacy or avoid the gaze of a social inferior.

With the advent of the railway age the majority of coaching inns underwent an abrupt decline. Staff were paid off, rooms were not cleaned and standards were generally lowered in a long decline towards the end of the century. Many inns which had boomed during the coaching era were sold and became private houses, or the property of the brewers. Even the supporters of the railways could not boast of their successors the railway hotels, which were either Gothic monstrosities or jerry-built edifices close to the stations themselves.

Yet in 1861 a Frenchman M. H. F. Esquiros could still give a pleasing verbal picture of a modest village inn:

'Near a pond on which geese are flapping or ducks diving stands an old house over which a vine twines its vigorous arms. This tree is happy and does not regret its native country. A trough, ever full, invites the horses to rest and dip their thirsty mouths in the sparkling water. A rusty sign hanging from an iron rod allows you to guess at a portrait half-effaced by rain. Here everything breathes the calmness and – may I use the expression – the good conscience of the house . . . From (it) you can see the church, the gravestones, the school round which the children buzz and the common on which they sport. The public house keeps up in English villages the social link between men separated during the greater part of the day in the solitude of the fields. They meet at night to talk about wheat, hops and races; a few innocent games of chance, or raffles, occupy their leisure hours to the great amusement of the simple and hard working men who laugh at trifles.'

By the end of the 19th century, traffic on the roads had begun to develop once again, with the advent of the motor-car. Already some inns had opened their doors eagerly to the bicyclists, but none could have foreseen the developments in store in the twenties and thirties, let alone in the second half of the twentieth century. As late as the Edwardian era there were still many inns and alehouses which had changed little in essentials from those visited by Byng, Moritz, or even earlier travellers. There were too many pressures at work for them to remain unchanged much longer.

Chapter Five

Alewives, Innkeepers, Ostlers and others

Alewives – Licensing – Magna Carta – Peg Measure – Ale Conner's Oath – Breeches – Brewer's Soul and the Devil – Marked distinction between Brewers and Alehouse Keepers – Beer and Ale – Beer Brewers – Hops – Burton Ale – Harrison on Innkeepers – On Ostlers and Thieves – Torrington Diaries – Puritans – Survey of Twenty-Six Counties – Newark to Doncaster – York to Wigan – Leicester to Bristol – Izaak Walton

A nose he had that gan show,
What liquor he loved I trow,
For he had before long seven yeare,
Been of the town the ale-conner.

ANON: *c.* 1380.

THROUGHOUT THE DEVELOPMENT of alehouses, inns and taverns certain figures have always been prominently associated with them, although their roles have changed somewhat over the ages. The early alehouse keepers were, of necessity, their own brewers and brewed their own ale on the premises, often in very primitive conditions. As early as 1189 an injunction by the City Council of London decreed in part:

'that all alehouses be forbidden except those which shall be licenced by the Common Council of the City at Guildhall . . . And that no . . . alewife brew by night, either with reeds, or straw, or stubble, but with wood only.'

Apart from the indication that a form of licensing was already being enforced the inference is plain that brewing at this time was regarded as essentially a woman's task. Only in the seclusion of all male ecclesiastical establishments where no woman supposedly penetrated was it regarded as a suitable male occupation. With the superior facilities available to them, however, the ale produced in the monasteries was a good deal superior to most of that produced in the generally less well built and less well managed surroundings of the average alehouse. It was, indeed, famed throughout Europe.

Controlling the standards of ale brewed and the measures used was one of the principal concerns of the authorities from the earliest days. Thus in 1215 one of the Articles of Magna Carta signed by King John at Runnymede, Number 35, stated significantly: 'There shall be standard measures for wine, ale and corn . . .' Subsequently an Assize of 1277 decreed: 'No brewster (i.e. female brewer) shall henceforth sell except by true measures, viz: the gallon, the pottle (or half a gallon) and the quart . . . the tun to be 150 gallons.'

The methods of measurement were probably fairly rough and ready since it was not even easy to estimate individual amounts drunk due to the habit, still common in the 14th century, of passing ale round an alehouse in a large wooden tankard marked with wooden pegs inserted at regular intervals of about half a pint. This device originated during King Edgar's reign in the 10th century as a means of controlling excessive drinking. Like many such attempts it had precisely the opposite effect to that intended and resulted in competitive drinking, hence the sayings 'Have a peg' and 'Take him down a peg'. Alternatively the marks were sometimes called pins, hence 'Merry as a pin' and 'Pin drunk'. Such communal drinking from the same cup remained common until towards the end of the 19th century.

As a check on alehouse brews and measures an official known as the ale-conner, or ale-taster, was appointed in the second half of the 14th century in London and this example was followed throughout the rest of the country in the 15th century. Part of the oath of office for ale-conners in the City of London in 1377 read:

'You shall swear that you shall know of no brewer or brewster who sells . . . otherwise than by measure sealed and full of clear ale . . . and that so soon as you shall be required to taste any ale of a brewer or brewster shall be ready to do the same; and . . . shall set a reasonable price thereon according to your discretion . . . nor when you are required to taste ale, shall absent yourself without reasonable cause and true . . .'

Whenever an alehouse had finished preparing a fresh brew of ale they would hang an alestake, a stake thrust through a sheaf of barley from which latterly hung a garland or wreath of evergreen, as a signal to the ale-conner that his services were required to test its strength and pass it fit for sale. Thus the ale-conner soon became a familiar and important minor official in the later Middle Ages.

As well as tasting the brew and assessing its strength and appearance the ale-conner had certain standard tests. It is said that part of his garb was a pair of leather breeches, a mark of his calling, because it was standard practice for him to pour a measure of ale on a wooden bench and sit down on it conversing and drinking for half an hour. If at the end of that period his breeches stuck to the bench this indicated too high a sugar content and accordingly sub-standard ale, whereas if his breeches were free it was regarded as good ale.

Despite his no doubt permanently stained leather breeches, the ale-conner, the forerunner of the Customs and Excise Official, had considerable power, but that power was restricted to the town, or city, over which the Council nominating him had control. It was further restricted by Common Law. The King's Forests, often considerable areas of land, came under Forest Law, which was quite separate and distinct. Similarly lands owned by the Church, again large tracts of country, were governed by Ecclesiastical Law. It was not unknown for alehouses to set up in defiance of the Council on such land abutting the town, but outside their jurisdiction. This in turn forced the Councils to decree it illegal to bring beer or ale into the town from outside, or otherwise tie themselves in knots. Furthermore it resulted in considerable variations in standards and measures.

There can be little doubt the ale-conner's task was no sinecure for there are many references in mediaeval poetry to the fraudulent brewers and bakers, giving short measure, or providing poor ale. The stock joke was of the Devil, when the souls were being released, begging to be allowed to keep one and being given the soul of a brewer. William Langland also wrote:

'Women that bake and brew . . . harm the poor and privily and oft they poison them. They grow rich . . . they become landlords. If they sold honestly they would not build so high . . .'

It was during the 15th century that the distinction between brewers and alehouse keepers first began to be marked. In 1437 the Brewers Company was incorporated by Royal Charter. In 1446 the Mistery of Hostelers was formed, but in 1473 changed their name to Innholders. Finally in 1493 the Beer Brewers were recognised as a Guild. Thus it is apparent that the Innkeepers by this time recognised themselves as a separate body, as did the Ale Brewers and the Beer Brewers, who even had separate measures. An ale barrel held 30 gallons, a kilderkin 15 gallons, whereas a beer barrel held 36 gallons, a kilderkin 18 and a firkin 9 gallons.

Since 1400, hops had been imported from Holland to make beer, and as they were to some extent a preservative, there was not the same danger of the brew going sour before it had been sold, once the barrel had been tapped. By 1524, Flemish emigrants were growing hops in Kent and, in London at least, beer was regarded as an accepted drink. Somewhere around 1550 the Ale and Beer Brewers joined forces to form one Brewers Company, although this was not finally accepted officially until 1556.

As early as 1542 there is a reference to a Henry Leake, who employed more than ten people in brewing beer and not only supplied his own alehouse, but also supplied others as well. By 1561 the records show that his son was employing eighteen people and his output was measured in hundreds of barrels annually. The Leake family seem to have been among the first families to become wealthy as brewers. Although considerable argument was to continue about the relative merits of ale and beer the new brew was to be the foundation of the brewers enhanced fortunes in the years to come.

There is a traditional schoolboy's mnemonic which runs:

'Hops, Reformation, Bays and Beer
Came to England all in one year.'

Although wildly inaccurate, like many such abbreviations of fact, the combination of hops, beer and the Reformation had a considerable effect on brewing, inns and ultimately on drinking habits during the ensuing centuries. Not only were many old hostels and ecclesiastical establishments converted into inns in lay hands, but many of the dispossessed clerics turned to brewing or innkeeping as the only trades they knew. In private hands some of the old ecclesiastical brews began to find a wider public.

For a long time hitherto, for instance, Burton Ale had been known for its particular excellence. This was due to the special qualities of the water there, which contained calcium sulphate and magnesium salts, without which good bitter ale or beer cannot be brewed. From the Reformation onwards it began to be sold in increasing quantities. As early as 1630 Burton Beer was being sold in London at 'Ye Peacocke' in Gray's Inn Lane and was in great demand by the visitors to Vauxhall Gardens.

Whether it was due to the fresh admixture of clerics in their ranks or the new converted hostels, William Harrison was very complimentary in 1563 about the inns and their standards in his *Description of England*, as we have seen. He also spoke highly of the innkeepers:

'It is a world to see how ech owner of them (the inns) contendeth with the other for goodness of intertainment of their ghests, as about finesse and change of linnen, furniture of bedding, beautie of roomes, service at table, costlinesse of plate, strengthe of drinke, varietie of wines, or well using of horses.'

On the other hand Harrison had dark suspicions about the treatment of the traveller's horses by the ostlers:

'(His) horses in like sort are walked, dressed and looked unto by certain hostelers, or hired servants, apppointed at the charges of the goodman of the house, who in hope of extraordinarie reward will deale verie diligentlie after outward appearance in this their function and calling. Herin nevertheless are many of them blameworthie in that they doo . . . deceive the beast oftentimes of his allowance by sundrie meanes . . .'

He also had some strong words to say on the subject of chamberlains (i.e. the male forerunners of chambermaids), and tapsters, (i.e. barmen, who tapped the barrel and drew the ale or wine), whom he considered were often in league with thieves lying in wait for travellers:

'Certes, I beleeve not that a chapman or traveller in England is robbed by the waie without the knowledge of some of them.'

He mentioned the ostler who always tried to feel the weight of a traveller's bag or travelling wallet carried on the saddle, or, if this failed, the chamberlain who always tried to move it in the bedchamber on the pretext that it was more convenient elsewhere, so that they could get an idea of whether he was carrying valuables or not. He also warned against letting the tapster see how much money the traveller was carrying when he bought drinks. He ended by indicating that it was; 'an hard matter to escape all their subtile practices.' Not content with this he added a final word of warning to unwary 'ghests':

'Some think it a gay matter at their coming to commit their budgets (i.e. wallets) to the goodman of the house; but thereby they oft bewraie themselves. For albeit monie be safe for the time it is in his hands (for you shall not hear that a man is robbed in his inne) yet after their departure the host can make no warrantie of the same; his protection extendeth no further than the gate of his own house; and there cannot be any surer token unto such as prie and watch for those booties, than to see anie ghest deliver his capcase in such a maner.'

In some cases, it may well be, these warnings were unfortunately necessary. The 16th century was not notable for its lack of footpads, or highway robbers, and there have always been some inns known for their unsavoury connections with highwaymen, just as others were known for their strong links with smugglers at a later date. On the whole, however, the honesty of the average innkeeper was above reproach and since their business was dependent on their reputation most of them were careful only to employ honest servants. As there was no shortage of labour this was not a difficult matter. Any ostler, chamberlain, tapster, or other servant, down to the potboy, who ran between cellar and bar with pots of ale or beer, suspected of such behaviour was simply discharged on the spot.

A description of travel in 1585 contained in the Torrington Diaries leads one to the conclusion that some ostlers and chamberlains must have been above reproach:

'In my last return from Edenborough in Scotland, coming homeward through Yorkshire, I travelled somewhat out of the common high London way, or purpose to see the countrie – And one day among others, towards even, I chanced to come to a little thorough fare town call'd Rippon, where at the very ent'ring into the town I met a poore old woman, of whom I asked if there were any good lodging in the town; she answered me that there was lodging at the Signe of the Great Omega – And thither I went and ent'ring into the house, I found in the hall, the goodman, his two sonnes, his chamberlain and his hostler singing the CIII Psalme of David very distinctly and orderly; the goodwife with her two daughters sat spinning at their wheeles a little distance from them.

'So I bade them God speed. The hoste very curteously arose and bade me welcome; so did the wife also, and asked me whether I meant to tary all night. I answered yea – Then he asked me if I would see my chamber. No gentle hoste (quoth I) I will not hinder so much your good exercise, for I am sure I cannot be lodged amisse in this house. Not so, sir (quoth he) but ye shall have the best that we have and welcome. I gave him hasty thanks. Then he enquired of mee, of whence I was, where I had been and whether I was bound. I tolde him I was a southern man borne and dwelling and that I had been at Edenborough in Scotland; and was thus farre in my way homeward. In good time, sir (quoth he) and yee are hartely welcome into this part of Yorkshire. I thank ye, gentle hoste (quoth I) &c &c.'

Such Puritan innkeepers and their families were probably rather exceptional, although at that time there was no religious or social stigma attached to keeping an inn or brewing. Indeed subsequently some of the leading brewers came from Puritan or Quaker antecedents. However there can be very little doubt that ostlers as a class were guilty only too often of giving the horses short rations and pocketing the difference since Fynes Moryson also echoes Harrison's warning about them.

Either because they were experienced travellers, or more probably because they looked after their own horses, the Captain, Lieutenant and Ensign from Norwich never mentioned this particular hazard during their *Survey of Twenty-Six Counties in a Seven Weeks Journey* in 1634. They did, however, give some good examples of the varied types of innkeeper, both male and female, whom they encountered, also some occasional glimpses of the waiters and others who attended them. Although obviously young and lighthearted they were interested in seeing as much of each town and city they visited as possible in what was by the standard of the times a whirlwind tour. In most cases they found their innkeepers to be extremely helpful guides. Indeed at this time and as late as the end of the 18th century, as Byng indicates, this seems to have been accepted as one of the innkeeper's duties to his guests when so required.

Their first night out from Norwich they arrived late at their Inn, the Antelope, in Lincoln, where they found their host had 'bouz'd it soe' he was already in bed. The next day, however, they found his charges very cheap and 'his Hostship wondrous merry', which almost inclined them to stay. Nevertheless they continued to Newark, arriving tired out, but were greatly entertained by their Host 'with mirth, merry tales and true Jests as made our weariness clean forgotten'. The day after, in typical August weather, they were thoroughly soaked with rain during their day's ride and on arriving at Doncaster recorded:

'Took up our lodging at the Three Cranes where we found a grave and gentile Hoste (no less you can imagine him to be having so lately entertayn'd and lodged his Majestie in his Progress) . . . Our Hoste was an Alderman and in his Worship's Inn we were as soundly drench'd at our first entrance as some Scotch Gentlemen were we fell upon by the way. We joyned our Forces English and Scottish together that night and being well ayr'd and dry'd we had good free mirth; and made it serve with Yea forsooth and No forsooth from these young Gallants. The next morning we arose to be gone, but these Scotch Blades had so weary'd themselves and their Galloping Galloways that forced they were to rest there a day or two.'

On their next day's journey to York they were once again soaked to the skin and appear to have arrived very wet and weary, but luckily for them they found an even better inn, as they noted:

'We most happily and fortunately lodged in Coney Street . . . at the house of a Loving and Gentile Widdow, who freely and cheerfully extended her bounteous Entertainment to us; for no sooner heard she of her wet and weary, benighted Guests, but she came to us and welcom'd us with a glass of good Sacke and a dish of hot fresh Salmon, she herself presenting both in that timid and modest Family phrase of the Northern speech Marry God thank yee for making her house our harbor and likewise tooke such care of us both at Board and Bed as if she had been a mother, rather than our Hostesse . . .

'(After seeing round York the next day) . . . it was time to hasten to our good Hostesse and her good Ordinary, who would not be forgot, for such in our Southern parts cannot be afforded under three times the price. The Company and discourse was answerable to the Cheere; for such an Ordinary, such Usage, such an Hostesse and such good Company we shall hardly find the like in the whole Island . . . With many Marry God thanke hers we bad our Cheap Hostesse Adiew . . .'

In Durham they stayed at the Lion. They termed their host 'an honest trout' and commented on being well 'attended by his She-Attendants'. It would appear that, although female innkeepers were common enough, chambermaids, rather than chamberlains, were not yet so common. Strangely enough, while in Yorkshire they do not appear to have tasted the famed Nanny Driffield's Ale, nor, while in the neighbourhood of Newcastle, the strong ale known as Stingo for which it was then more widely famed than for coal. At this time most areas took pride in their own

Interior of an alehouse – illustrating an old ballad 'Jack Hard-hand's Lamentation' : c. 1628

Sunday afternoon in a Gin Palace : 1879

LOUSE HALL.
MOTHER LOUSE, of LOUSE HALL, near OXFORD.
ou laugh now Goodman two shoes, but at what?
y Grove my Mansion House, or my dun Hat;
s it for that my loving Chin & Snout
re met; because my Teeth are fallen out;
Is it at me, or at my RUFF you titter;
our Grandmother you Rouge nere wore a fitter.
Is it at Forehead's Wrinkle, or Cheek's Furrow,
Or at my Mouth, so like a Coney-Borrough,
Or at those Orient Eyes that nere shed tear,
But when the Excisemen come, that's twice a year.
KISS ME & tell me true, & when they fail,
Thou shalt have larger Potts & stronger Ale.
THREE LICE PASSANT
Engraved from the Original Print by David Loggan — Price 7.6.
Pub^d. by C. Johnson.

Interior of a country Inn

ales and at Wigan when they were invited to take a morning draught on Sunday with their hosts and some friends it turned out to be:

'A Whiskin (i.e. measure) of Wiggin Ale, which they as heartily and merrily whisk't off as freely and liberally as they call'd for it. It was as good as they that gave it, for better Ale and better Company, no Traveller whatsoever could desire . . .'

A few days later, still pressing on doggedly, they recorded:

'Wee gott by Noone to the Harte in Derby where with a hearty and merry fatt Hostesse we dyned. We had so little time of stay here that we could not taste of the nappy Mother Ale (Mother Penwakers) of all these parts, but parted speedily from her (in a Cup of good wine).'

Outside Leicester they lost their way and only arrived 'with the help of a fortunate guide'. They stayed at the Angel, an expensive and 'a majesticall inn' where they encountered 'an intelligible Chamberlayne' who acted as their guide to the town. They then went on to Hereford:

'Wee entered that old City and billeted ourselves at a proper and portly Alderman's House, an Hoste both of Qualities and Reckoning; for the former his breeding shew'd it, for the latter our Purses have cause to remember it . . . he was both an able and willing Intelligencer and a good Discourser and of a civill and gentile Garbe. The next morning our Hoste march'd with us out of his own Ward and shew'd us the whole City . . . We discharg'd our hard Reckoning and shook not our Hands, but our Heads at our deare Worshipfull Hoste and away . . .'

In Gloucester they stayed at the 'new Inne', which they noted was 'much frequented by Gallants' due largely to the Hostess 'as hansome and gallant as any'. Her husband was away 'travelling at the charge of other Travellers'. Their last halt was in 'Bristow City' (i.e. Bristol), where they lodged at Gilliards Inn 'with Mr. Hobson, a grave, proper, honest and discreete Hoste', lately mayor of the City and so they thought, 'A man more fit for such a place than such a House'. Yet in spite of this double-edged comment they seem to have fared well, except for 'one of his hungry domesticke servants, who no sooner saw us every meale, but scar'ed us into an Eating Feaver'. Finally 'with a Cup of Bristowe milke we parted'.

From the tenor of their journal it is obvious they must have been

Royalist supporters and one wonders what happened to them during the Civil War eight years later. The four years of the Civil War and the inevitable turmoil involved must have been a particularly trying time for the inn and alehouse keepers with both sides billeting their troops upon them and no doubt causing endless damage and trouble. During the Puritan regime which followed, and the manifold restrictions on their activities involved, life cannot have been much easier.

From Izaak Walton's *Compleat Angler* written in 1653 we get a glimpse of an inn under the Puritan regime. It is said to have been The Thatched House in Hoddesdon, Hertfordshire, about which Piscator informs Venator:

'I'll now lead you to an honest Ale-house, where we shall find a cleanly room, lavender in the windows, and twenty ballads stuck about the wall. There my hostess, which I may tell you is both cleanly and handsome, and civil, hath dressed many a fish for me; and shall now dress it after my fashion and I warrant it good meat.

'Come hostess, how do you do? Will you first give us a cup of your best drink and then dress this Chub as you dress'd my last, when I and my friend were here about eight or ten days ago?'

It was under the Commonwealth regime that regular coach travel started on the roads, between 1650 and 1660. One of the first regular coach services was from London to Chester, which took six days. Another, from London to Exeter, took eight days. Even Oxford at that time was considered a two-day coach journey from London, but the very fact that traffic was growing on the roads was a sign of better times ahead for the innkeepers. With the Restoration, the life of the country, and of the inns and alehouses in particular, at once became freer and easier.

Chapter Six

Brewers, Landlords, Chambermaids and others

Pepys – Drawers – Mrs. Aynsworth – Ale-Conners – Gaugers – Chasm between Brewers and Alehouse Keepers – Michael Combrine – John Richardson – Moritz – Waiters and Chambermaids – Landlord – Byng – Inns and Ostlers – Eating and Service – W. Kitchiner – Duke of Wellington's Act – Sporting Brewer and Red-cheeked Landlord

Come Landlord fill the flowing bowl
Until it doth run over,
For tonight we'll merry, merry be,
For tonight we'll merry, merry be,
For tonight we'll merry, merry be-e-e
And tomorrow we'll be sober.

Traditional: Drinking Song.

FROM PEPYS'S DIARIES, as always, some clear pictures of the everyday life of the times are available. He described the scene on a journey from Cambridge to London very vividly:

'27th February 1660: Up by four o'clock . . . Mr. Blayton and I took horse and straight to Saffron Walden, where at the White Hart we set up our horses and told the maister of the house to shew us Audley End house; who took us on foot through the park and so to the house . . . which . . . was exceeding worth seeing . . . After that I gave the man 2s for his trouble and went back again . . . So we went to our Inn, and after eating of something and kissed the daughter of the house, she being very pretty, we took leave . . .'

He describes a scene in a London tavern in the same year as follows:

'September 21st, 1660 . . . To the Hope Taverne and sent for Mr. Chaplin, who with Nicholas Osborne and one Daniel came to us and we drank off two or three quarts of wine, which was very good; the drawing of our wine causing a great quarrel in the house between the two drawers, which should draw us the best, which caused a great deal of noise and falling out till the master parted them, and came to us and did give us a large account of the liberty that he gives his servants, all alike, to draw what wine they will to please his customers; and we did eat above two hundred walnuts. Nicholas Osborne did give me a barrel of samphire . . .'

Inn standards and charges varied enormously and coach travel was still extremely slow. Nor were all inns precisely what they seemed. The Reindeer at Bishops Stortford kept by Mrs. Aynsworth was a case in point. A noted procuress, she had been banished from Cambridge for her evil practices. When subsequently the Vice Chancellor and various heads of Colleges unwittingly stopped there for the night on their way to London they were royally entertained and fed off silver plate. In the morning she refused to make any charge maintaining that by banishing her from Cambridge they had made her fortune. Pepys recorded:

'7th October 1667 . . . and so, about nine o'clock, I and my wife and Willett set out in a coach I have hired with four horses . . . So we to Enfield and there bayted, (i.e. rested) it being but a foul bad day, and there Mr. Lowther and Mr. Burford, an acquaintance of his, did overtake us, and there drank and eat together; and, by and by, we parted, we going before them and very merry, my wife and girle and I talking and telling tales and singing and before night come to Bishop Stafford, where Lowther and his friend did meet us again and carried us to the Raynedeere, where Mrs Aynsworth, who lived heretofore at Cambridge and whom I knew better than they think for, do live . . . (She) did teach me "Full forty times over", a very lewd song . . . and is here as she was at

Cambridge and all the good fellows of the county come hither . . . here we stayed and supped and lodged . . . my wife and I in one bed and the girl in another in the same room and lay very well, but there was so much tearing company in the house that we could not see the landlady; so I had no opportunity of renewing my old acquaintance with her . . .'

Pepys comments when he had occasion to make the same journey the following year indicate the swiftness of developments in coach travel associated with the inns. They also indicate the unchanging reticence of the English traveller. He wrote:

'23rd May 1668: Up at four o'clock . . . with my boy Tom, whom I take with me, to the Bull in Bishopsgate Streete, and there, about six, took coach, he and I and a gentleman and his man, there being another coach with as many more also in it, I think; and so away to Bishop Stafford. Dined and changed horses and coach at Mrs Aynsworth's; but I took no knowledge of her . . . Here and at London nothing but rain, insomuch that the ways are mighty full of water, so as hardly to be passed. I hear Mrs Aynsworth is going to live in London, but believe will be mistaken in it; for it will be found better for her to be chief where she is, than to have little to do in London. After dinner to Cambridge about nine at night . . . well pleased all this journey with the conversation of him that went with me, who I think is a lawyer and lives about Lynne, but his name I did not ask.'

During the period from the first imposition of a tax on beer in 1642, and for the next hundred years or more, the duties of the ale-conner were to be steadily superseded by the Customs and Excise official known as the Gauger, whose task it was to enter the breweries and gauge the vessels for taxation purposes. By this time the ale-conner's duties had come to include such allied activities as control of the markets, and their posts were either not renewed or changed to Clerk of the Market or similar titles. Gradually, like old soldiers, the ale-conners faded from the scene, while the Excise Gaugers, armed with the right of search and confiscation, busied themselves with the ramifications of the breweries, also with attempting to thwart the activities of the Free-traders or uncovering unlicensed stills or similar nefarious practices affecting non-payment of duty or tax.

Throughout the same period a steady and far reaching evolution was taking place in the brewing trade. The division between brewers and ale-house keepers, already quite distinct was to become even more marked, indeed a clear-cut chasm. At first the division was most marked in

London, where the competition from cheap spirits was soon affecting many alehouse keepers extremely adversely. As early as 1686 a report of the Commissioners of Excise referred to the alehouse keepers' severe straits: 'Most of them being in debt to the brewers and living on their stocks.' Inevitably, when the alehouse keeper went bankrupt, the brewers found themselves as the principal creditors owning the property. The more they lent or advanced stock to bolster up their own outlets for their beer the more inevitable the process became. As the pressure from cheap spirits increased so the process developed momentum. Due to the increasing competition of other brewers it was essential to keep the retailers in business, even if it meant owning them and running them as 'tied' houses. So the process snowballed.

The records of Samuel Whitbread, founded in 1742, indicate that in 1746 the brewery owned thirteen alehouses and by 1756 the number had already risen to twenty-four. Throughout the country as a whole the process was a good deal slower than in London, but as the century advanced the larger breweries found it essential to own more alehouses to ensure outlets for their products. Gradually the large brewers found themselves expanding to keep pace with their own production.

Throughout the 18th century it seemed as if the various governments were intent on forcing the brewers to make their fortunes. In 1756 they received a further boost when a tax was placed on brewing victuallers on the same scale as the common brewer. The amount was only thirty shillings on brewers of not more than a thousand barrels a year, but it seems to have had considerable effect. It is significant that the number of brewing victuallers, or alehouse keepers who brewed their own ale or beer, dropped by nearly ten thousand in the period between 1748 and 1758, with the figures thereafter showing a steady decrease. The estimated totals of beer produced remained constant or rose only very slightly during the same period so that the ten thousand decrease represented to a large extent so many more customers for the brewers.

Apart from these aspects the most notable development of the 18th century from the brewers' viewpoint was the publication of the first books revealing full details of the 'mysteries' of brewing. Hitherto these had always been closely guarded secrets handed down from father to son, or from mother to daughter. When a brewer, Michael Combrine, published his book *An Essay on Brewing* in 1761 it was the first of its kind. He revealed such finer points as the use of isinglass finings for clarifying beer. In 1784 followed *The Philosophical Principles of the Science of Brewing*, by another brewer, John Richardson, who emphasised the importance of the hydrometer, or saccharometer, and the thermometer in the brewing process. In particular he pointed out the use of the hydrometer for testing the worth of a sample of malt or the strength of a brew for the first time. The way was clear for brewing as a scientific industry to make further steady progress.

The final nail in the private brewer's coffin was driven home when Lord North, in order to raise further finance for the American War of Independence, nearly doubled the tax on a bushel of malt and withdrew the right of private maltsters to compound their duty with the Treasury. This meant that the private brewer was forced to pay the same rates as the commercial brewer. Inevitably, as Adam Smith had foreseen by taxing beer direct it led to an increase in revenue, but it equally led to an immediate decrease in private brewing. It seemed as if the 18th-century governments were deliberately encouraging the commercial brewers by driving their private competitors out of business.

To return to the inns and their retainers, we find Pastor Carl Moritz fuming over the behaviour of the waiters and others at an inn in Windsor in 1782. He wrote:

'As I entered the inn and desired to have something to eat, the countenance of the waiter soon gave me to understand that I should find there no very friendly reception. Whatever I got, they seemed to give me with such an air, as shewed too plainly how little they thought of me; and as if they considered me but as a beggar. I must do them justice to own however, that they suffered me to pay like a gentleman. No doubt this was the first time that this pert bepowdered puppy had ever been called on to wait on a poor devil who entered their place on foot. I was tired; and asked for a bedroom, where I might sleep. They showed me into one, that much resembled a prison for malefactors. I requested that I might have a better room at night. On which, without any apology, they told me they had no intention of lodging me, as they had no rooms for such guests; but that I might go back to Slough, where very probably I might get a night's lodgings . . . They made me however pay them two shillings for my dinner and coffee . . .'

When he did eventually find a room at an inn in Windsor for the night he was not much better treated. However, on the following morning when leaving, he managed to get his own back on a particularly insolent waiter and chambermaid. He described the scene, which was typical of the times, as follows:

'As I was going away, the waiter who had served me with so very little grace, placed himself on the stairs and said: "Pray remember the Waiter". I gave him three halfpence; on which he saluted me with the heartiest G—d D—n you, sir, I had ever heard. At the door stood the cross maid, who also accosted me with – "Pray remember the chamber-maid." "Yes, yes," said I, "I shall long remember your most ill-mannered behaviour and shameful incivility," and so I gave her nothing. I hope she was stung and nettled by my reproof; however she strove to stifle her anger by a contemptuous, loud, horse laugh. Thus, as I left Windsor, I was literally followed by abuse and curses.'

His description of an encounter he had with a landlord at an inn near Derby indicates that after a great number of rebuffs he had learned the most tactful approach. It also indicates that the habit of drinking to someone at this period still involved sharing the tankard with them, a method of drinking going back to the days of the Saxons or earlier. As Moritz pointed out, since he did not like the beer anyway, this suited him perfectly:

'This inn was called *The Bear*: and not improperly; for the landlord went about and growled at his people just like a bear, so that at first I expected no favourable reception, I endeavoured to gentle him a little by asking for a mug of ale, and once or twice drinking to him. This succeeded; he soon became so very civil and conversible that I began to think him quite a pleasant fellow. This device I learned of the Vicar of Wakefield who always made his hosts affable by inviting them to drink with him. It was an expedient that suited me also in another point of view, as the strong ale of England did not at all agree with me. This innkeeper called me, Sir; and he made his people lay a separate table for himself and me; for, he said, he could plainly see I was a gentleman . . . I . . . observe that the English innkeepers are in general great ale drinkers; and for this reason most of them are gross and corpulent; in particular they are plump and rosy in their faces.'

Byng, with his greater discernment and knowledge of the English inn, had some pertinent remarks to make about innkeepers. He was often intolerant, but, as already noted, when he found satisfaction he gave it due notice. He also, more to the point, gave his reasons and they were generally sound. In a tour to North Wales in 1784 he recorded:

'The Talbot Inn at Hartlebury is just such a one as horse travellers shou'd stop at, and what I always seek; where the whole family are employed in your service, for the maid new dresses herself, the boy is detach'd to the butchers and bakers, and the mistress acts as cook . . . It was quiet, cheap and pleasant.'

He had a reactionary objection to the new turnpike roads, which were improving the means of travel at a considerable rate. He was also not given to suffering fools gladly. He frequently commented on the general lack of information innkeepers often had of their own area and on a ride into the West he noted:

'I had much discourse with the landlord and hostler about my road, of which they were equally ignorant; and in regard to places worth seeing, enquiry is only to be made in London; – more devoid of information two people could not be; The country is only improved in vice and ignorance by the establishment of the turnpikes – The hostler however derided my looking into my maps, saying that such sort of things could give no information.'

He obviously shared both Harrison and Fynes Morison's views on ostlers and, for that matter, his views on waiters and chambermaids were not much better. In 1784 he observed:

'Having a most particular dislike to the company of a servant on the road I detach'd him forward to prepare for me and my horses proper accommodation at night. This is the true use for servants on the road, tho' but seldom what their masters require of them; trusting to the waiter and chambermaid for dirty glasses and ill made beds and confiding the care of their horses to drunken, roguish hostlers while their own genteel followers are regaling themselves in the genteel parlour the horses are neither clean'd nor fed.'

On the subject of service at meals in inns he contrasted the arguments of a friend of his and his own, painting an appalling picture of the general standards of service, which it is only fair to assume he coloured somewhat to lend substance to his viewpoint:

'He chooses when at meals to have the waiter (commonly a woman) attend behind his chair, and hand to him everything he wants; now my way wou'd be to get everything necessary; beer, wine, water etc. etc. upon the table before dinner; then dinner being serv'd, I say to the waiter. "You need not stay, I will ring when we want you" and now let us talk our talk and eat our meat at leisure.

'Instead of a nasty, dirty wench, watching you all the time, picking her nails, blowing her nose upon her apron, and then wiping the knives and the glasses with it; or spitting and blowing upon the plates. Surely with a great fortune, there is nothing so comfortable for a small company as dumb waiters; as for myself, I am uneasy when a fellow stands behind me, watching me, running away with my plate, and winking at his fellows.

'At my inn, particularly, when people come in tired, they are as greedy of food, as of venting their mind to each other of their past travelles and future intentions; and this they cannot do before attendants.'

Presumably because most of his journeys were far enough from London, Byng appears to make no mention of 'tied' houses and the effects of the ownership of such a house by the brewers. The numbers of such inns and alehouses increased greatly towards the turn of the century, particularly around London, and by 1816 nearly half of the 'victualling houses' in London were owned or controlled by the brewers. In towns close to London the situation was often even worse. For instance, in Reading only two of the sixty-eight inns and alehouses were not brewer controlled.

Inevitably this must have had a considerable effect on the standards of service since a landlord owning his own inn or alehouse generally tended to take a personal pride in the service he provided, whereas an employee manager or tenant was unlikely to have the same interest, nor was much incentive offered to him to do so. Admittedly there was little likelihood of disturbances or law breaking on such premises, since any such happening quickly resulted in the brewers taking drastic action, but that is another matter.

It is significant that in 1827, at the peak of stage-coach travel, in a guide for travellers entitled *The Travellers Oracle*, W. Kitchiner wrote:

'The elegance and magnificence of some English inns and taverns are equal to those of many noblemen's houses . . . but the generality of taverns, in our opinion, are rather to be endured than enjoyed.'

The gulf between brewer and innkeeper was now that of employer and employee or landlord and tenant. Throughout the late 18th and early 19th century the brewers had been growing increasingly wealthy. Most of the present well-known names in the brewing industry had already appeared and considerable fortunes were being founded. Faced with the Duke of Wellington's Beer Act of 1830, intended to break their stranglehold on the trade, the stock story is of the two brewers in the hunting field, who were heard to say that by the end of the season they feared they would have to sell their hunters and give up their sport. The following season, when the Act had been in operation for nearly a year, they were observed to be still hunting but mounted on vastly more expensive blood horses.

The net effect of the Duke of Wellington's Act, far from adversely affecting the brewers, was to depress the status of the inn and alehouse keeper even further by virtually opening the field to anyone, whether of good or bad character, who cared to pay two guineas for a licence to open a beer shop. Although this situation was to a large extent remedied in 1834 by reversion to the powers of the licensing justices to approve licences, the fact remained that until finally superseded in 1860 there were a great number of small beer shops competing with the old established inns and alehouses which inevitably drew away their custom. Combined with the depression following the collapse of the coaching trade many of the old inns were forced out of business and the innkeepers and staff reduced to seeking employment in 'tied' houses.

The cumulative legislation of the 19th century attempting to remedy the situations arising from the earlier Acts is in places hard to follow. Combined with the onslaught of the militant temperance movement the innkeepers must often have had a hard time to survive. However, with the backing of the brewers, survive they did and by the end of the century the situation was more stable.

It is not perhaps too much to suggest that one of the things both brewers and inn- or alehouse keepers shared with each other and with their customers, which helped them to survive, was a joint interest in sport. The brewers, aping their betters at the start of the century, had been a stock joke. By the end of the century the brewers were fully accepted in the highest society. The country innkeeper who did not gladly greet the hounds and the meet on his premises was not likely to remain in business long. Their country customers were all interested in country sports. It was these, as well as the desire to drink ale or beer which bound them together.

The hearty sporting brewer and the red-cheeked jovial landlord may be figures from a past age today, but they really did exist. Their customers in the country were of a like type. In London the situation might be quite different. The Industrial Revolution could lead to many changes there and in the major industrial towns and cities, but until the Edwardian age the countryside remained very much as it had been a hundred years or more before.

Chapter Seven

Inside the Alehouse, Inn or Tavern

Brew house – Curfew – Communal downstairs rooms – Taverns and Inns – Harrison – Fynes Morison – Mouth Tavern Stocklist – Heywood on drinking vessels – Thomas Tryon on Bottled Ale – Wine bottles and Port – Dr. Johnson – De la Rochefoucauld – Clubs and Assembly Rooms – Insurance – Moritz – Byng on old mansion – Priest Holes – Service at Coaching Inn – Loudon – Esquiros

If there's a Heaven, which I do not doubt,
There'll be an inn fire and a glass of stout.
If I can have just those two things
I'll do without my harp and wings.

WILLIAM BERNARD: Miscellaneous Verse: 1947.

IT IS PROBABLE that the earliest alehouses were very little different from the other buildings in the villages in which they were to be found. The interior itself would have been almost identical with any other; a bare earth floor and crude wooden furnishings with the cauldron in which the water for making the brew was heated almost certainly also used for cooking when not so required. Like any other woman in the village, when not preparing a brew, the alewife would require it for cooking for her husband and family. Although in some cases the house may have been adapted a little for the purpose, it is unlikely that any were built, at least in the earliest days, specifically as alehouses.

Only as the population increased and the demand for ale grew accordingly, were buildings likely to be adapted especially for selling ale rather than primarily as living quarters. Then gradually a room, or outhouse, might be set aside especially for brewing the ale, with a cauldron devoted to that purpose alone. The downstairs room where the ale was dispensed might then be fitted out with rather more benches to accommodate the drinkers in wet or cold weather when they could not comfortably drink outside. With the growth of competition no doubt the alehouses were soon vieing with each other to attract custom. It would soon have been appreciated that the ale drinkers' comfort and entertainment was nearly as important as the standard of the ale itself, perhaps even more so.

As we have seen, it was the monasteries which gave the lead in the matter of ale brewing. It was probably there that the importance of keeping ale at a steady temperature was first appreciated. Once it was fully understood that hot weather made ale go sour more quickly, the advantages of a cellar would soon become apparent. However, it is unlikely that such refinements were introduced until well into the Middle Ages. By that time brewing was being conducted in some places, particularly in the monasteries, on quite a considerable scale and even in ordinary alehouses special cauldrons and brew rooms would be set aside for the brewing process. Leading off from this would be the main room set aside for drinking and entertainment, which probably opened in its turn directly onto the street for convenience of access.

Although there were no official opening or closing hours for alehouses or taverns, it must be remembered that all mediaeval townspeople were subject to curfew, after which honest people were expected to remain indoors. In spite of the widespread superstition and fear of the dark common then this was quite clearly often ignored. A proclamation of 1329 stated categorically:

'Whereas misdoers going about by night have their resort in taverns more than elsewhere and there seek refuge and watch their hour for misdoing, we forbid that any taverner or brewer keep the door of his tavern open after the hour of curfew . . .'

Only alehouses and taverns are mentioned because until later in the century it is doubtful if any inns as such existed. As we have seen they began primarily as rest houses to take the overflow when the need arose from the hospices and hostels introduced by the ecclesiastical establishments for pilgrims and other travellers. Some were merely converted taverns or alehouses, but others were probably modelled on the hospices and hostels themselves. Apart from cellars and brew houses and all the appurtenances of an alehouse, they would also have large communal rooms downstairs for the guests and bedchambers for them upstairs. There would also be stabling for horses attached, probably built around a courtyard at the rear.

In theory, the tavern, being principally concerned with wine, would not be as large as the inn, although it, too, would have cellars and communal downstairs rooms. Theoretically it would have neither stabling nor bedchambers since it was concerned only with the sale of wine and the entertainment of the guests. In practice, as we have seen, there was often considerable difficulty in distinguishing between an inn and a tavern and no doubt the larger tavern was very hard to tell apart from the smaller inn.

It was in these large communal downstairs rooms that most of the life of the inn centred. Here the strolling players, jugglers, contortionists and acrobats beloved of the mediaeval world performed for the entertainment of the guests. Here, in front of a blazing fire in winter time the guests drank their draughts of ale or wine and told stories and sang late into the night. Only the wealthy or the nobility withdrew to their private chamber upstairs.

By the 15th and 16th centuries the grander inn was quite an impressive building with a courtyard, timbered galleries, stables and barns for fodder behind it. The outbuildings would also include a privy, an oven house, a brewery and a still-room. There would be a large ground floor room facing the street and a Parlour as well as a general reception room hall which might also serve as a dining-room for meals with the cellars beneath it. Such names as the Entry Chamber, the Flower de Luce Chamber, the Peacock Room and similar rather charming individual names would be given to the bedchambers on the first floor. Above them would be the garrets or cock lofts where the servants slept.

The kitchen would be one of the most important rooms in the house. It would be lined with copper pots, pans and kettles, pewter and brass plates and basins and candlesticks. There would be a large stone mortar, several cauldrons with pot-hooks for the vast fire, tongs, griddles and large frying pans and steamers of iron. A large wooden table would dominate the centre of the room and the beams of the ceiling would be hung with hams, sides of beef, bacon and other meats. The pantry near at hand would be filled with drinking vessels from leather jacks to pewter pots and tankards, glasses and goblets.

As the table manners of the average Englishman improved so the general feeding arrangements became more elaborate, graduating from wooden trenchers and plain wooden tables to plate and linen. Fine damask tableclothes and napkins for each guest would be provided. In his *Description of England* of 1563 William Harrison recorded:

'Our innes are also very well furnished with naperie; for beside the linnen used at the tables, which is commonlie washed dailie, is such and so much as belongeth unto the estate and calling of the ghest. Each commer is sure to lie in cleane sheetes, wherein no manne hath been lodged since they came from the landresse. . . .'

Fynes Morison, some fifty or sixty years later in his *Itineraries* described the alternatives open to the guest at an inn of the period:

'If he will eat with the Host, or at a common table with others, his meale will cost him six pence, or in some places four pence (yet this course is less honourable and not used by Gentlemen); but if he will eate in his chamber, he commands what meat he will, according to his appetite, and as much as he thinks fit for him and his company, yea, the kitchen is open to him to command the meate to be dressed as he best likes; and when he sits at Table the Host or Hostesse will accompany him, or if they have many Guests, will at least visit him, taking it curtesie to be bid to sit downe; while he eates, if he have companie especiallie, he shall be offered musicke, which he may freely take or refuse, and if he be solitary the Musitians will give him the good day with musicke in the morning . . .'

The choice of wines available in the average inn at this period, early in the 17th century, would have been considerable. Some idea of the choice is to be had from the stock inventory of the Mouth Tavern in Bishopsgate Without kept by George Hitchecock in 1632, as follows:

'Imprimis fower pipes (1 pipe = 115 gallons) of white wine	£20	0s	0d
Item, two hogsheads of old Graves wine	2	0	0
Item, seven hogsheads of Orliance wine	17	10	0
Item, one butte of Malligo wine	17	0	0
Item, one ranlett of Sherry Sacke contayning sixteene gallands	1	12	0
Item, three-quarters of a pipe old Malmsey	1	10	0

Item, one-third of a pipe of Malmsey	£5	0	od
Item, three gallands of Alligante, at 3 sh. per gall.	0	9	0
Item, halfe a pipe of Malligo wine	6	0	0
Item, one hogsheade of old Clarett	0	16	0
Item, one hogshead of Graves wine	3	0	0
Item, half a hogsheade of white Orliance wine	2	10	0
Item, half a hogshead of Graves Claret	0	10	0
Item, one thyrd part of a hogshead of red wine	1	10	0
Item, three tunne and a half of emptye hoggsheads at 6s per tunne	1	1	0
Item, three Rochelle pipe, emptye		9	0
Item one Alligant pipe, emptye	0	3	0
Item to dusson (2 dozen) and eight bottles of ale	0	5	8
Items, one cane and funnel for wyne	0	1	8'

This rather startlingly varied selection of wines and bottled ale could be drunk from an equally surprising selection of drinking vessels at this time. A very full list of both the various drinking utensils and the plates and dishes available is provided by Heywood's *Philocothonista, or the Drunkard opened, dissected and anatomised* written in 1635. This reads:

'Of drinking cups, divers and sundry sorts we have, some of them of elm, some of box, some of maple, some of holly, etc.: Mazers, broad-mouthed Dishes, Noggins, Whiskins, Piggins, Crinzes, Ale-bowls, Wassail bowls, Court Dishes, Tankards, Kannes, from a pottle (quart) to a pint, from a pint to a gill. Other bottles we have of leather, but they are mostly used amongst the shepherds and harvest people of the country; small Jacks (i.e. leather drinking mugs) wee have in many alehouses of the Citie and suburbs, tip't with silver, besides the great Black Jacks and Bombards at the Court, which when Frenchmen first saw, they reported at their return into their country that Englishmen used to drink out of their boots: We have besides, cups made out of horns of beasts, of cocker-nuts, of goords, or the eggs of ostriches; others made of the shells of divers fishes. Come to plate, every tavern can afford you flat bowles, beer bowles, beakers; and private householders in the citie when they make a feast to entertain their friends, can furnish their cup boards with flagons, tankards, beer cups, wine bowles, some white, some purcell gilt, some gilt all over, some with covers, others without, of sundry shapes and qualities.'

It is interesting to note that bottled ale was included in the inventory

Owing to thefts by the 'Man with the carpet bag', people carrying carpet bags were looked on with suspicion

"DIP YOUR ROLL IN YOUR OWN POT AT HOME."

Room in the Coach and Horses, Bartholomew Close

18th-century billiards

of the stock of the Mouth Tavern as early as the 1630s. Bottle making had been recognised as a trade as early as 1373, but the bottles then had been of leather and used simply as a means of carrying liquor from a cask to the table, or on journeys. The early glass bottles of the 17th century were squat, clumsy creations and it is not clear when they were first used for bottling ale. Records indicate that very considerable quantities of ale were bottled and laid down in cellars during the 17th century, but as late as 1691 we find Thomas Tryon in *The Way to Health, Long Life and Happiness* inveighing strongly against bottled ale:

'It is a great Custom and general Fashion nowadays to bottle Ale, but the same was never intended by any true Naturalist that understood the inside of things. For tho' Ale be never so well wrought or fermented in the Barrel, yet the Botling of it puts it on a new motion or fermentation, which wounds the pure Spirit and Balsemick Body; therefore such Ale out of Bottles will drink more cold and brisk, but not so sweet and mild as the same Ale out of a Cask, that is of the proper Age. Besides the Bottle tinges or gives it a cold, hard quality, which is the nature of Glass and Stone, and being the quantity is so small, the saturnine nature of the Bottle has the greater power to tincture the Liquor with its Quality. Furthermore all such Bottle Drinks are infected with a yeasty furious foaming matter, which no Barrel Ale is guilty of . . . For which reasons Bottle-Ale or Beer is not so good nor wholesome as that drawn out of the Barrel or Hogshead; and the chief thing that can be said for Bottle-Ale or Beer is that it will keep for longer than that in Barrels, which is caused by its being kept, as it were, in continual motion, or fermentation.'

It was precisely because of its keeping qualities that bottled ale or beer became increasingly popular and during the 18th century was readily obtainable in any inn, alehouse or tavern. By this time the alehouses were becoming more sophisticated. In the better alehouses the standards of furniture and entertainment were improved in an effort to draw custom away from the cheap gin shops which were the bane of the first half of the 18th century. Benches, tables and chairs would be provided for customers and bowling alleys, cards, dice and even shovel-boards would be available for their amusement. In the cruder establishments, the mere tippling houses, there might still be an earth floor, but the overall standards had considerably improved throughout the country.

In the taverns in the latter half of the century the wine bottle underwent a slow metamorphosis. In the early 18th century it had been unfit for laying down in a cellar. By the 1770s it was more suitably shaped, though longer in the neck and shorter in the body than the modern bottle. In 1775 the first vintage port was produced and in 1787 a French bottled vintage claret of Chateau Lafitte followed. By the early 19th century the modern shape of bottle had emerged and port and wine was being laid down in cellars throughout England.

Thus, Dr. Johnson, who boasted of drinking three bottles of port and being none the worse for it, never drank vintage port. The wine he drank was more akin to burgundy, without the body of the vintage port. Nor were the bottles as large, so that three bottles then was roughly the equivalent of one or one and a half in the following century. However, Dr. Johnson was a stout supporter of the inn and tavern. Boswell quoted him as follows:

'In contradiction to those who, having a wife and children, prefer domestic enjoyment to those which a tavern affords, I have heard him (Johnson) assert that *a tavern chair was the throne of human felicity*. As soon (said he) as I enter the door of a tavern, I experience an oblivion of care, and a freedom from solicitude; when I am seated I find the master courteous, and the servants obsequious to my call, anxious to know and ready to supply my wants; wone there exhilerates my spirits and prompts me to free conversation, and an interchange of discourse with those whom I most love; I dogmatize, and am contradicted; and in this conflict of opinions and sentiments, I find delight.'

Dr. Johnson was undoubtedly a man fond of inns and for that matter of English drinking habits. They did not always strike a foreigner as being quite so attractive. De la Rochefoucauld in particular was revolted by the ancient English custom of drinking to each other from the same drinking utensil, which was to persist until the end of the 19th century. He expressed himself forcibly by his standards on the subject:

'There is one thing that must strike everyone and that is the common habit of all drinking beer from the same glass, even if there are twenty at a table. When you ask for a drink some fresh beer is poured into the old at the bottom of the glass and you have to drink or let it pass. Moreover this dirty and revolting custom has become so well established that it has become an act of politeness at a ball for example to drink beer or punch or some other beverage after a lady has drunk from the same glass to show that you do not mind her leavings. This may be all very well on some occasions, but there are some ladies with whome I should not care to indulge in this form of politeness.'

De la Rochefoucauld, however, admired an institution common to many inns at that period. Throughout the country there are still to be seen many of the fine Assembly Rooms as they were termed which were frequently built onto Inns at this time. In these spacious and often extremely well designed and elaborately decorated Georgian rooms, dances, banquets and other public meetings would be held. De la Rochefoucauld commented particularly on various associations which met there: he noted:

'These are associations of people interested in, and enthusiasts for, the same branch of art, or some subject suitable for discussion. They fix one day of the week, or sometimes of the month, and spend it to discuss together the progress of the subject which is the raison d'etre of their association. Their meeting place is an inn, where they arrive for dinner; they talk at table until seven or eight; tea and a light supper make the evening pass quickly and the party breaks up reluctantly; the time seems short and there is no sign of weariness. I admit that I have observed that sometimes the conversation was not confined to the subject forming the basis of the society and that hunting and women are often subjects of conversation between labourers and gentlemen-farmers who ought to be thinking about their ploughs . . . It is to be noted that these frequent meetings of little societies put money into circulation and encourage the innkeepers to have their rooms very clean and even introduce a slight measure of luxury into their establishments. In towns . . . the large inns reap an advantage . . .'

De la Rochefoucauld also noted the establishment of a form of club which is still in various forms to be found today. He referred to this as only applying to 'small labourers, whom we call peasants': 'The meeting place is an inn, but a village inn, or the smallest inn in a town. There the club meets for dinner once a year. The price of the dinner is fixed; not so low that it could not be cheaper, but not high enough to ruin the company as a whole. The English always conduct their business round a dinner table; it is there that they are happiest and most liberal. These clubs are to be found in every part of England; every country district derives some benefit from them. On the inn in which the meetings are held there is a box locked with two keys; with a little slot into which club members put their money. The innkeeper is always a member and keeps one of the keys, the other is kept by some one well known in the neighbourhood.'

'The members pay into the box every week a sum calculated on the average length of human life towards providing the three or four shillings a week which the club provides to its sick members. When a member is ill he sends his wife to fetch the money from the club. As is right and proper his sickness must be sufficiently severe to prevent him from working. He receives three or four shillings during the whole of his illness.'

Whereas de la Rochefoucauld was interested in the social aspects of the inn, that other foreign observer of the same period, Carl Moritz was more observant of the actual interior itself. He described the kitchen of one inn he visited, where he was duly fed, in terms which bring it to life:

'The chimney in this kitchen, where they were roasting and boiling seemed to be taken off from the rest of the room and enclosed by a wooden partition; the rest of the apartment was made use of as a sitting- and eating-room. All round the sides were shelves with pewter dishes and plates, and the ceiling was well stored with provisions of various kinds, such as sugar loaves, black puddings, hams, sausages, flitches of bacon, etc.'

Strangely enough, although he stayed in countless inns during his many peregrinations around the country, it was seldom that Byng really bothered to go to the length of describing them in any detail. On one exceptional occasion, however, even he showed himself reluctant to leave an inn and he went on to describe it in such terms that one can readily understand his feelings. It was during 1787 on a tour to North Wales when he encountered this paragon amongst inns. He wrote:

'Kept on to Broadway . . . and did put up at a most comfortable, cleanly house, the White Hart, where a delicious loyn of veal was ready to be served and I was ready for eating it; which I did in ample quantity, and then had a superabundant temptation by an apricot tart; nor could I determine upon going away . . . There cannot be a cleanlier, civiller inn than this is, which bears all the marks of old gentility, and of having been a manor house; walls very thick, floors oaken and wide, and the remains of much tapestry, for carpeting, whereon is well told instructive church history. My bed room was very large, with black oaken boards, a wrought ceiling, a wide cornice, with a lofty mantlepiece; in short I appeared to be in the grand bedchamber of an old family seat – In the kitchen hung a picture, which appear'd to me the work of a great master . . . Nor are their charges unreasonable as you may perceive by the following bill: Tea 9d: A chicken &c 2s: Tart (Apricot) 2d; Liquors 2s 3d: Breakfast 9d: Total 5s 11d.'

In an old inn converted from a country house, such as this, there might well have been a priest hole, or similar hidden room. From the 16th to the 19th century many inns acquired such secret rooms, or hidden passageways for a number of reasons, generally connected with breaking the law. Apart from secreting priests, a hideaway for contraband spirits or for free-trading accomplices anxious to escape the attention of the Excise men was often useful. In inns and taverns in ports or near the coast subject to periodic visitations from the Press-gang there were often hidden cupboards, or attics, or convenient exists by which the customers might escape the clutches of the navy. During the rebuilding prevalent in the Georgian era it was simple to add such a room or a convenient means of ingress or exit and many are still to be seen.

With the tremendous development of the coaching services during the early part of the 19th century a new sense of urgency entered the world of the inn. Coaches had to be provided with fresh horses, the coach passengers served with food and drink, all within a set time, in order not to hold up the service. Inevitably the passengers must have suffered considerable discomfort at times. Trying to drink scalding hot coffee and somehow at the same time eat sufficient to last until the next chance of a meal cannot have been easy during the short time allowed them.

The scene at many such well known sporting and coaching inns must often have been an interesting one. When overnight stage-coaches made their halt for breakfast at dawn they would expect to find steak and kidney pies, bacon and poached eggs, toast and muffins, coffee and tea, all steaming hot and a cold side table of hams, rounds of cold beef, pigeon- or game-pie, and loaves of household brown bread on wooden trenchers with Stilton or Cheshire cheese beside them. Gentlemen in pink coats on their way to a meet of hounds, passengers from the stage-coach muffled in many coats and scarves and chilled with cold, and possibly the passengers from a passing post-chaise might all be gathered together round the breakfast table eating their way noisily through the meal and each trying to attract the attention of the harassed waiters and serving maids. Some might be calling for brandy, the coachman himself possibly for gin or rum, or purl, a hot beer mixed with gin, but most would be asking for mulled ale to keep out the cold. Then the signal for time would be called and everyone would reluctantly return to the coach to move on once more, leaving the hunters and the post-chaise travellers in comparative peace.

Writing in 1833 J. C. Loudon in his *Encyclopedia of Cottage, Farm and Villa Architecture* gives an exact account of what he would expect in his inn of that date:

'Inns in a wealthy and highly civilised country like England contain all the luxuries of a private mansion; and the traveller who stops in them with plenty of money, may enjoy many of the comforts of home without its cares . . . The inn contains an entrance hall, in which there always ought to be a porter to announce the arrival of guests, by ringing one bell for the hostler, and another for the waiter; an ante-room or stranger's room, into which the guests are first shown, and where they are waited upon by the master, mistress, or some upper servant, to ascertain the sort of accommodation they desire. A complete inn ought to have large rooms for parties to dine in on public occasions, or in which may be held public meetings, assemblies, balls, etc; it ought to have suites of apartments, consisting of one or two sitting rooms, one or two bedrooms, a maid-servant's, or nurse's room, and a water closet, such suites of apartments being frequently required in first rate inns, by wealthy families who travel with their own carriages and horses, and who wish to live at an inn as privately as if they were at home. There ought to be suites or apartments for single persons consisting of a bedroom and sitting-room each . . . The Bar, or Office of an Inn being its characteristic feature, it is proper that it should be shortly described; its situation ought to be central in the interior of large buildings, commanding views of the front entrance hall and back entrance; and as far as possible, of the foot of the principal staircase, and looking along the principal passages . . . Here the books of the Inn are kept, and orders given to the cook, the keeper of the cellar, the ostler, or the stable yard keeper, and here also all monies are given in . . .'

He contrasted the inn with a private house as follows:

'An inn differs from a private dwelling house chiefly in having certain apartments and stores open to the public generally. In a private house all is private; but in an inn, one of the recommendations to the traveller is to see a well-stored larder, and a spacious public room, in which he may take his meals, either at a common table, or a separate table . . . Inns and Public Houses for the country . . . include various degrees of accomodation, from what is found in the small hedge ale-house, to what is afforded by the mansion inn, with its spaces for amusements, garden, farm and perhaps park. In all of them the object is to provide entertainment for the public . . .'

Loudon, however, was writing at the peak of the stage-coach era and, as we have seen, throughout the latter half of the 19th century the inns suffered a steady decline. Yet the interiors remained little changed.

M. Esquiros in 1861 pictured the inside of a modest village inn very similar to many found today, as follows:

'The interior is clean tidy and merry; an entrance hall with pewter pots arranged along a plank fastened to the wall and to which a vigilant hand has given the lustre of silver; a parlour of whitewashed walls, a floor gilded with fine sand, wooden benches and tables, and old clock, which enlivens the room with a monotonous tic tac, engravings representing historical scenes, or the likeness of Wellington, and an old chimney in which the coals crackle and the cricket sings, windows in which an unknown hand has engraved a motto on the glass.'

Chapter Eight

Outside the Alehouse, Inn or Tavern

Roman signs – Ale-Stake – Middle Ages – Richard II – Charles I – White Hart at Scole – Red-paint on alehouses – M. Misson's comments – John Taylor – Individual Signs – Moritz at Nuneham – Byng – Legislation – Coaching Age – Assembly Rooms – Bowling Greens – Highwaymen, Dick Turpin, Duval – Maclean – Spence Broughton – Mrs Hues – Coach held up with Candlestick

I'm amazed at the signs
As I pass through the Town
To see the odd Mixture:
A Magpie and Crown . . .
The Tun and the Lute
The Eagle and Child
The Shovel and Boot.

The British Appollo: ANON: 18th century.

THE ROMANS USED signs to indicate to a largely illiterate population the purpose of their shops, as is known from excavations at Pompeii and elsewhere. The vine and ivy leaves, symbol of Bacchus, were used to indicate a wine shop. When entertainment could be had within, in the form of draughts, a chequer-board sign would be shown. During their lengthy occupation of Britain it is virtually certain they brought this custom with them, although like many others it may have lapsed on their withdrawal from the country. This seems unlikely, however, since, as we have seen, the first known sign for an alehouse was the ale-stake and barley sheaf. This was used from the 14th century onwards to indicate that ale had been brewed and to summon the services of the ale-conner. Later on the ale garland of greenery and hops intertwined in a wreath was hung outside the alehouse. The tavern selling wine displayed an evergreen bush, hence the saying 'good wine needs no bush'.

Apart from the ale-stake, as we have seen, there would have been virtually nothing to distinguish the early alehouse from the buildings around it. Where there were a number of alehouses in one town the problem of differentiating between them caused their owners to erect signs to identify them. Amongst the earliest of these was possibly the Chequers, also such easily identifiable objects as the Sun, the Moon, the Stars or the Plough. The illiterate peasant could thus readily agree to meet his companions at the sign of the Sun, or whichever alehouse he preferred.

Throughout the Middle Ages such signs and the ale-stick and bush were the outward indication of the alehouse or tavern. As early as 1375 it was decreed that no alehouse should have a sign extending more than seven feet over the highway. From this it would appear that even at this early date the inn sign was proving a nuisance and a hazard to travellers. Yet in Richard II's reign, in 1393 an edict was issued making it compulsory for alehouse keepers to display a sign:

'Whosoever shall brew ale in the town with intention of selling it must hang out a sign, otherwise he shall forfeit his ale.'

As the inns became popular during the 15th and 16th centuries they too adopted signs of similar kinds, such as The Tabard at Southwark. With the more elaborate signs developed by the wealthier inns no doubt the hazard to passers-by became even greater. The problem seems to have been a fairly continuous one, but it finally began to get completely out of hand in the 17th century. In 1625 in a Charter for the City of London, Charles I permitted the use of hanging signs. Unfortunately the Charter failed to make any regulations regarding their size, with the result that soon signs of vast size were appearing as innkeeper vied with innkeeper for custom.

In 1655, perhaps anticipating the Restoration, James Peck a Norwich merchant erected a remarkable sign outside his inn the White Hart at Scole in Norfolk at a total cost of £1,057. Sir Thomas Browne described this famous sign in 1663 as follows:

'I came to Scoale, where there is a very handsome inne, and the noblest signpost in England about and upon which are carved a great many stories as of Charon and Cerberus, Actaeon and Diana and many others; the sign itself is a white Hart, which hangs down carved in a stately wreath.'

This expensive work of art seems to have been crowned with a weather-vane and to have stretched clear across the road outside the inn. At the time it was the wonder of the neighbouring counties and people even made journeys especially to see it. To that extent it certainly seems to have served its purpose in attracting custom to the inn and no doubt James Peck did not regret the £1,057 he spent on having it built, even though this was an unheard of sum to spend on such a purpose in those days. Yet it was not long before similar vast signs spanning the road outside an inn were commonplace, though few were as elaborate or expensive. Most consisted of large cross beams with the inn sign hanging from it.

The development of the inn sign seems to a large extent to have eclipsed the alehouse signs. During the 16th and 17th centuries they appear to have used red paint to denote their premises. By long established usage the windows of an alehouse facing onto the street seem to have been without glass and unshuttered, but were covered with a lattice to screen the drinkers inside from the view of the passers-by. At this period it was customary to paint these lattice screens with red paint.

Prior to the Civil War there seem to have been a very considerable number of alehouses in some areas as a much quoted comment by Decker in 1632 mentions: 'A whole street is in some places but a continuous alehouse, not a shop to be seen between red lattice and red lattice.' It was also possible at this time to refer to someone being: 'as well known for his wit as an alehouse by a red lattice.'

Despite an Act in Charles II's reign attempting to curtail the size of inn signs there was no effective legislation on the subject and throughout the 17th and 18th centuries the signs continued to grow in size and ostentation. A Frenchman, M. Misson, writing in 1721 of a visit to England, commented:

'At London, they are commonly very large, and jut out so far, that in some narrow streets they touch each other; nay and run across quite to the other side. They are generally adorned with carving and gilding; and there are several that, with branches of iron which support them, cost above a hundred guineas . . . Out of London and particularly in villages, the signs of inns are suspended in the middle of a great wooden portal, which may be looked upon as a kind of triumphal arch to the honour of Bacchus.'

Throughout the 17th and 18th centuries, as is the case still, the subjects of inn signs and the names of the inns changed frequently. John Taylor, who has already been quoted, was a strong Royalist and for his uninhibited attacks on the Parliamentarians had been made a Yeoman of the Guard. In 1645 he took an inn at Long Acre named 'The Crown', which he renamed 'The Mourning Crown'. This was not unnaturally regarded as 'malignant' and he was offered the choice of removing it or being charged with treasonable conduct. He then, characteristically, replaced it with 'The Poet's Head' and his own portrait, including the words on one side:

> 'There's many a head stands for a sign
> Then, gentle reader, why not mine?'

On the other side:

> 'Though I deserve not, I desire,
> The laurel wreath, the poet's hire.'

He also issued one of his typical rhyming pamphlets publicising his inn, which included the lines:

> 'Now if my picture's drawing can prevayle
> 'Twill draw my friends to me, and I'll draw ale,
> Two strings are better to a bow than one;
> And poeting does me small good alone.
> So ale alone yields but small good to me,
> Except it have some spice of poesie.'

Such highly individual signs are rare in any age, but subjects for inn signs have always been legion. Often they are related to historic events, thus The Royal Oak refers to Charles II's escape after the battle of Worcester, when he hid from his pursuers in an oak tree at Boscobel. The King's Head is another favourite sign, generally relating to the death of Charles I. The various Kings and Queens of England, from Alfred onwards, but particularly perhaps King Henry VIII and Queen Elizabeth are favourite choices, especially if there is any local connection, however remote, with them in the district. The Wars of the Roses, both Lancaster and York, are commemorated in many inn signs around the country. It is also common practice throughout England to adopt the coat of arms and sometimes the name of the local large land-owning family as the sign of the inn.

Inevitably sport played a great part in the naming of country inns, since sport has always been an integral part of the country way of life. Thus The Fox and Hounds, The Horse and Hounds, The Greyhound, The Dog and Gun, The Anglers, The Cricketers and many more such signs are directly related to the sports of the countryside. Other such names as The White Hart, The Boar, The Bear and The Fighting Cocks relate, of course, to sports of the past. The Wheatsheaf, The Lamb, The Fleece, The Ox, The Plough and others of a like nature are even more directly related with the countryside and country living.

Yet the origins of inn names are not always as simple as they may seem at first sight. On the contrary they can often be extremely obscure, or have their roots in some local incident, as in the case of Byng's favourite inn, The Haycock at Wansford. In this instance the story goes that a hay-making yokel suffering from the effects of too much strong ale and hot sun went to sleep on a haycock by the side of the river some miles upstream. The river overflowed and carried him, still sleeping soundly on his hay-cock, down to Wansford Bridge, where he awoke to find himself bumping gently against the bank. Seeing an interested spectator on the bridge looking down at him, he demanded to know where he was. On being told Wansford, no doubt still somewhat fuddled, he asked 'In England?' Another version has the yokel being carried out to sea from Wansford, but this stretches the bounds of credibility somewhat.

John Taylor learned this story in his travels and could not let it pass without rendering his own rhyming version as follows:

'On a haycock sleeping soundly
The river rose and took me roundly
Down the current; people cried
As along the stream I hied
"Where away" quoth they, "From Greenland?"
"No, from Wansford Bridge in England." '

By the late 18th century the inn signs had reached their zenith in size and costliness. Pastor Carl Moritz commented frequently on their size, noting particularly: 'the amazing large signs hanging suspended over the street from great beams; they have the appearance of gateways, but the whole apparatus is intended for nothing more than to tell the inquisitive traveller that there is an inn.'

Yet in the days before street lighting there was something to be said for such signs, as Moritz himself found on his journey to Oxford:

'When I reached Nuneham I was not a little tired; and it was also quite dark. The place consists of two rows of low, neat houses, built close to each other, and as regular and uniform as a London street. All the doors seemed to be shut; and even a light was to be seen only in a few of them. At length, quite at the end of the place, I perceived a great sign hanging across the street, and the last house to the left was the inn, at which everything seemed to be still in motion . . .'

Regrettably the size of the inn sign has never borne any relation to the standard of hospitality offered and once again Moritz found himself turned away with the door slammed in his face, although he was to end the night carousing comfortably with the dons at Oxford in the Mitre. Byng, of course, was far too experienced a traveller to judge an inn by its exterior, or by its sign, but even he from time to time was constrained to comment on the size of a particular specimen as on his arrival at Rugby in 1789 where the Earl of Warwick's famous crest formed the subject matter in this instance:

'A most tremendous sign of the Bear and Ragged Staff invited us into a very alehouse; tho' the best of the town . . .'

Towards the end of the 18th century the situation had got out of hand and quite apart from the danger to human life when they collapsed, or blew down in high winds, such signs were very often serious obstructions to travellers in carriages or to waggoners and their loads. In 1797 the first effective legislation was passed compelling the removal of any such signs which impeded movement on the street or pavement, or were likely to cause danger to passing travellers. The result was the removal of most of the old archway signs spanning the road, although the process throughout the length and breadth of the country was a slow one and a few still remain even today.

With the growth of travel the Canal, Coaching and Railway Ages each left their mark on the inns and alehouses with such names as The Navigator, The Grand Junction, The Coach and Horses, The Highflyer, and latterly The Locomotive and The Railway Arms. With the growing pride of the artisan many alehouses also appeared with names such as

The Mason's Arms, The Bricklayer's Arms and The Miner's Arms. The war with France and nationalistic ardour also produced such names as The Trafalgar, The Lord Nelson, The Waterloo and The Duke of Wellington. The Volunteer, The Militiaman, and many more stem from much the same source. Sufficient instances have been given to indicate the numerous and varied origins of the inn and alehouse signs which depended ultimately, as still today, on the individual imagination and choice of the innkeeper himself.

During the late 18th and early 19th centuries with the advent of the coaching age, the inns on the main coaching routes developed their stabling facilities, their coach-houses, their barns and their outbuildings to a hitherto unprecedented degree. Many old Tudor oversailing frontages were modernised with Georgian red-brick flat facades. Thatched roofs frequently gave way to tiles or slates. Regency bow-fronted windows sprouted on old Queen Anne or Jacobean buildings. Palladian porticos and arched coach entrances to stable yards were added along with massive Assembly Rooms, often uneasily incorporated in the old building or attached to one side or the rear. Only from behind were the miscellaneous roof levels, the galleried courtyards and such features as oriel windows a clear indication of the true age of an inn.

In one of his tours into Sussex in 1888 Byng gives a picture of the sort of developments which were taking place. He also indicates unconsciously the importance to the inn of having the village green adjacent:

'Hawkhurst: our inn the Queen's Head of nice aspect . . . everything was neat and comfortable . . . we walked half a mile to the green . . . (where) was a well play'd single wicket cricket match; for the *gammsters* were expert – one man bowled excellently and a young man of gigantic stature was an excellent fieldsman . . . In this inn has lately been built a new large room for quarterly assemblies; and at the back of it is a neat and pleasant bowling green maintain'd by subscription; about which we walked with our conversable landlord . . . and I drank somewhat more than enough of port wine . . .'

The advantages of being adjacent to the village green where so many sports were played was very considerable from the innkeeper's viewpoint. Suitable land for a bowling green, or for skittles or other sports was also a considerable asset. In some districts where fives was keenly played, notably in the West Country, the inns even went to the extent of erecting special fives walls for the benefit of their customers and tournaments against neighbouring villages were organised. Covered skittles or bowling alleys adjacent to the inn were also built in some places and some reference to such attractions was often included on the sign in front of the inn.

One feature of the times, which most innkeepers would have much preferred to regard as in no way connected with their inns, but which was unavoidably bound up with the entire business of travel and at least in the public mind connected with them, was the highwayman. The highwayman's exploits gripped the public mind and imagination to a far greater extent than any other form of robbery. Something of the glamour of the cavalryman and the foxhunter perhaps attached itself to him, however petty his thefts. Pastor Moritz, ever ready with information he had gleaned on his travels, informs us that pickpockets were regarded as the highest order of thieves, but:

'Next to them, come the highwaymen, who rob on horse-back; and often, they say, even with unloaded pistols they terrify travellers, in order to put themselves in possession of their purses. Among these persons, however there are instances of true greatness of soul; there are numberless instances of their returning a part of their booty, when the party robbed has appeared to be particularly distressed and they are seldom guilty of murder.'

On the face of it this was not much praise, but the public imagination had been touched by feats such as Dick Turpin's famous ride to York, which has featured in prose and verse. The point that is largely overlooked is that in reality Dick Turpin was principally a horse-thief and deer poacher, who inclined to burglary on the side, rather than a highwayman to any great degree. No doubt he deserved his posthumous fame, but few other names of noted highwaymen survived the century, except possibly that of Claud Duval, another plausible rogue.

Captain Maclean, son of a clergyman, whose most famous exploit was holding up Horace Walpole, was primarily intent on securing himself an heiress when not 'on the road'. William Page and Spence Broughton, both sons of farmers, each suffered from a weakness for women. Page had a very similar career to Captain Maclean, but was more successful. He drew up a useful map of the roads around London and worked them from a phaeton, adopting different wigs and coats as his disguise and pretending to have been robbed himself. Broughton admitted a weakness for hazard, a game of dice similar to craps, and claimed to have lost £1,500 at it. All were duly hung and left in chains as was the custom.

One other, whose name may have been remembered if nothing else, was Jack Rann, or Sixteen String Jack, as he was nicknamed due to his flamboyant habit of having eight different coloured strings on each leg of his breeches. Starting life as a postillion he graduated to life on the road, but he seems to have been a boastful, rather unpleasant character and well merited his fate, ending like the others in chains on the gallows.

Not all were male. In 1810 a pamphlet referred to: 'The apprehension and taking of Mrs. Hues, the noted Female Highway Robber, aged twenty-eight years in the City of Bath . . . On Saturday 31st March, 1810, on the highway from Chepstow to Bristol, mounted on a fine bay gelding, dressed as a gentleman, and armed with brace of pistols, she rode up and attacked Mr. Whitecombe of the Boar's Head, Bristol, and with one of her pistols cocked, demanded his money instantly, or he was a dead man; he complied with this demand and gave his pocket book, containing 200 Guinea bills and a bank note, value 20 pounds. With this booty she took the road to Bath, but being closely pursued she was apprehended in that City. On examination she owned herself to be a woman and that her husband was a capital farmer near Chippenham, which proved true.'

Alas, she already had a criminal record for robbing a shop in Bath in 1806, for which she had been sentenced to seven years transportation, but for which she had been pardoned. She had then subsequently spent a year in gaol for a similar offence and she was also wanted on two other charges. She too was bound to end up on the gallows, but it is difficult not to have a certain curiosity regarding her background, about which there seems a painful lack of information.

It is true that sometimes the highwaymen relied on bluff and the natural fears of the travellers. Two bankers travelling from London to Norwich in 1812 agreed that though the coach had been held up several times recently they would not be overcome without a struggle. On Thetford Heath a figure loomed out of the darkness and challenged the coach, the moonlight glinting on the brass of the pistol he seemed to be holding. There was an exchange of words, the traveller warned that he was going to shoot and fired, but the coach did not stop. At Thetford the encounter was reported and on searching the Heath the assailant's body was found still holding the brass candlestick with which, in collusion with the driver, he had previously robbed the coach successfully.

Perhaps after all it is understandable that inns today should boast of their connections with highwaymen. It is certainly understandable that there is an inn named The Dick Turpin and another The Highwayman. With the passing of the coaching era they too had had their day. Robbing a mail train is not quite the same thing. Yet to hang in chains from a gibbet before graduating to an inn sign hanging outside an inn seems an irony of fate for any highwayman.

Loading the stagecoach in the yard of The Old Angle Inn : 1747

Sunday morning; waiting for the pub to open

'A Game of Four-Corners' by H. Carter

No. 51

'Ratting' in The Graham Arms

S

Chapter Nine

The Indoor Sports

Dice – Backgammon – Minister Northbrooke – Cotton – Hazard – Gaming Act – Cards – Puritans – Victorians – Origins of Handicap – Restoration – Byng – Draughts and Dominoes – Pepys – Strutt – Shovel-board – Shove-groat – Billiards – Troul-in-Madame – Bagatelle – Pin tables – Cock-fighting – Gervase Markham – Hidden room for illegal mains – Skittles and Nine-pins – Devil-among-the-Tailors – Ring the Bull – Darts – Quoits – Plays

An Englishman's a man of Parts,
He likes his beer and game of darts.
Should anyone his choice deplore,
'Twas thus for centuries or more.

WILLIAM BERNARD: Miscellaneous Verse: 1947.

AMONGST THE EARLIEST of games played in alehouses, inns and taverns undoubtedly dice ranks as the oldest. Originating from a game played with knucklebones popular with the Etruscans this is probably another introduction for which we have to thank the Romans, since they were certainly keen dice players. During the 9th century there is no doubt that dicing was widespread, for it was during the reign of King Edgar (959–975), as we have seen, that the clergy were prohibited from playing with dice. By the 12th century John of Salisbury wrote of ten different dice games being played, although unfortunately he did not list them. It is thus not surprising that in 1250 Henry II was forced to repeat the prohibition against clergy playing with dice, at the same time prohibiting them from card-playing for good measure.

By the later Middle Ages such sophisticated variations had been introduced as an early form of backgammon, a game played with draughts and dice on a marked board, requiring a considerable element of skill. The earliest known illustration of a backgammon board appears in an illumination of the 14th century, by which time one may assume it was already well established. Although not known as backgammon until the mid-17th century it was a popular pastime throughout the country during the 15th and 16th centuries, when it was termed 'playing at tables' and was undoubtedly common in inns and taverns.

Despite the element of skill required in backgammon, as opposed to the pure element of chance in dice throwing, it seems likely that it was included amongst the games prohibited by Statute in 1326 by King Edward III as distracting his subjects from their martial exercises and practice of archery. The games listed included, as we have seen, cards and dice and 'games of chance', which was probably intended to include backgammon. On the other hand 'playing at tables' was not expressly included amongst the games prohibited by Statute until Henry VIII's reign. In any event from their constant repetition it is clear that these decrees can have had little real effect.

Even Minister Northbrooke writing in 1579 in his *Treatise Against Diceing, etc.* recognised the element of skill involved in backgammon, although he was unrestrained in his condemnation of dice:

'This arte is the mother of lies, of perjuries, of theft, of debate, of injuries, of manslaughter, the verie invention of the Divels of hell . . . Playing at tables is far more tollerable (although in all respects not allowable) than Dice and Cards are, for that it leaneth partlie to chance and partlie to industrie of the minde.'

The Puritans, of course, objected strongly to dice, or indeed to any such form of 'frivolity'. In the case of dice they probably for once had good reason. There can be no doubt that many fortunes were wagered and lost at dice over the centuries, especially at the game of Hazard, and, as we have seen, at least one highwayman, Spence Broughton, claimed that his downfall was due to a liking for it. Nor was his a solitary case by any means.

According to Charles Cotton, writing in 1674 in *The Compleat Gamester,* there were then seven games 'within the tables', mostly similar to backgammon, and three games of dice 'without tables', of which by far the most popular seems to have been Hazard, a game closely resembling the modern Craps, of which indeed it was the forerunner. Yet even Cotton, writing enthusiastically on the subject of Hazard and describing it as 'the most bewitching game that is plaid on the dice' was forced to end up, rather illogically:

> 'To conclude, happy is he that having been much inclined to this time-spending, money-wasting Game, hath took up in time, and resolved for the future never to be concerned with it more, but more happy is he that hath never heard the name thereof.'

In spite of Cotton's half-hearted warning Hazard continued to be a popular gambling game throughout the country and in most inns and taverns, even after it had been declared illegal by Statute under Queen Anne in 1710. It was not really until the Gaming Act of 1845 empowered the authorities to search premises that it finally died out. Thereafter the licensees appreciated that it was not worth their while to allow such games to be played on their premises, whereas before they might well have turned a blind eye.

Backgammon seems to have remained popular for most of the 18th century, but by 1800 its popularity had waned with the gradual rise in favour of card games such as whist. Thereafter to all intents and purposes it ceased to be a game frequently encountered in inns and taverns. Despite a revival of popularity towards the end of the 19th century it remained principally a game for the nursery and schoolroom, rather than for the inn or tavern. Such games as whist, picquet and cribbage had by then become firmly established in the inns and lesser games such as brag and nap in the alehouses.

Although cards were only introduced into this country in the 13th century, the clergy, as we have seen, were prohibited from playing with them as early as 1250. Thereafter they were always amongst the games prohibited by Statute along with dice. Predictably, Minister Northbrooke in his *Treatise against Diceing, etc* of 1579 waxed extremely strongly against them:

> 'The plaie at Cardes is an invention of the devill, which he found out that he might the easilier bring in idolatrie amongst men; For the Kinges and Coate cardes that we use nowe were in the olde time the images of idols and false Gods . . .'

One must do Minister Northbrooke the justice of assuming that he believed what he said. On the other hand anyone who believed that would believe anything that suited him. Unfortunately this was the case with most of the Puritan extremists and as late as the Victorian era the high-sounding phrase that cards were 'the inventions of the devil' was still being unctuously mouthed by their killjoy descendants, who had not yet invented bridge.

Minister Northbrooke's fulminations did not prevent Queen Elizabeth and no doubt most of her subjects from playing cards, principally a game called Primero, or subsequently a game called Maw, which were the fore-runners of poker. By the time Cotton was writing on cards in 1674 several games which are still being played were already common. Picquet, with almost identical rules to those in use today, was already well known. Brag, another game still played, was common, as was Slam, the equivalent of Nap today. Other games included such varied names as Gleek, Basset and Lanterloo. A primitive form of whist was also played, although not yet as popular as in its later form. There were many other variations of these games as we find from Pepys:

'19th September 1660: At noon I went to the Miter taverne in Woode-streete (a house of the greatest note in London) where I met W. Symons and D. Scobell and their wives . . . Here some of us fell to handycapp a sport that I never knew before which was very good.'

This game handycapp was a form of the card game Loo, but with this difference that the winner of one trick had to put in a double stake and the winner of two a treble stake and so on. Thus if six people were playing and the general stake was one shilling when a player won three tricks he gained six shillings, but had to put his 'hand 'i the cap', or the pool, four shillings for the next deal. Thus originated the term 'handicap'.

With the Restoration, cards received a great impetus in popularity, but it was not until Holye first produced his Treatise on Whist in 1737 that this game became amongst the most popular in the country. By the end of the 18th century it was played almost to the exclusion of all else. Byng was a keen whist player and several times mentions his pleasure in playing cards in the evening during his journeys. In his tour to the north in 1792 for instance he chronicled:

'Monday, May 28th, Sun Inn, Biggleswade . . . In the evening the weather, after much wind, turn'd into heavy rain; so I had only to write, to tea and to stable and to wish for some quiet society; wondering where

I saw chaise travellers, masters of their own time, not put up in such weather and be comfortable; instead of forcing thro' the storms and seeing poor post boys wet to the skin! Why, there is a good inn, with good coffee and good wine? Stay then, and play at cards and backgammon; and depart when the wind does not blow an hurricane and the rain fall a deluge.'

As Byng was seldom in a hurry his attitude was understandable, but it was clearly common practice to play both cards and backgammon in an inn towards the end of the 18th century. Backgammon might soon be on the wane, but cards were to remain part of the standard inn equipment for the entertainment of their guests. Towards the end of the 19th century whist itself might slowly give way to bridge, but in the alehouse brag, nap and cribbage retained their popularity.

Two games which were to become popular in inns, taverns and alehouses, but chiefly in the latter, were draughts and dominoes. Both are of uncertain origins the former possibly developed from an ancient Egyptian game and the latter possibly from a Chinese counterpart. Undoubtedly, however, draughts was the first to be played in this country and the first book on the subject was written in 1756, while Pepys casually mentions playing a game of draughts at an inn, as if this were a common occurrence, as early as 1660:

'27th February, 1660 . . . and so that night, the road being pretty good, but the weather rainy to Eping. Where we sat and played a game of draughts; and after supper and some merry talk with a plain bold maid of the house, we went to bed.'

Dominoes, on the other hand, did not become popular until the 19th century in this country. According to Joseph Strutt writing in 1801 in his *Sports and Pastimes of the People of England*; 'Dominoes seem to have been little known in England till towards the end of the 18th century, when it was imported from France.' It was not apparently until Spanish dominoes was introduced in 1879 that the game became really popular. By the end of the century it had far outstripped draughts in popularity and was amongst the most widespread of games, to be found in almost every public house with more than a dozen variants practised, including some with intriguing names such as Muggins, or All Fives, Matador, Bergen and Sebastopol.

Another popular game at the end of the 19th century in most public houses was Shove-halfpenny. This was really a smaller, humbler, variant of the game of shovel-board, which dates back to the 15th century, and may possibly have originated as the result of sliding heavy pewter platters up the length of the great tables of the day. By the start of the 16th century special shovel-boards, or shuffle-boards, were being built, some thirty feet in length and three feet wide. Flat metal weights were then slid along the smooth surface of the board with the object of passing a line near the end, or poising over the end itself. If they went over they fell into a trough and were not counted. Each player had four weights and they played alternately.

As early as 1532 the privy purse expenses show that Henry VIII was playing with Lord Rochford: 'My lord of Rocheforde won of the King at shovilla-bourde and betting at the game £45'. By the 17th century the game had so gained in popularity that no large house or inn was complete without its shovel-board. On 30th July, 1662 Pepys wrote:

'Thence with Captain Fletcher . . . to Woolwich expecting to find Sir W. Batten there upon his survey, but he is not come and so we got a dish of steaks at the White hart, while his clarkes and others were feasting of it in the best room of the house and after dinner playing shuffle-boards, and when at last they heard I was there they went about their survey . . .'

As late as 1801 Strutt mentioned:

'I have seen a shovel-board-table at a low public house in Benjamin Street, near Clerkenwell Green, which is about three feet in breadth and thirty-nine feet two inches in length and said to be the longest at this time in London.'

Of course shovel-boards were expensive to have made and took up a lot of room, hence why the game gradually went out of fashion in the 19th century and also why the smaller version of shove-groat, or slyp-groat, as it was at first known, was naturally more popular in humbler establishments. Strutt, in his rather priggish way, refers to it as a game 'confined to common pot-houses and only practiced by such as frequent the taprooms'. That it has quite as ancient origins as shovel-board is plain from Shakespeare's mention of it in Act I, Scene I of *The Merry Wives of Windsor*:

'Seven groat in mill-sixpence and two Edward shovel boards that cost me two shillings and sixpence each.'

According to Strutt it could be played on any table with lines cut or chalked on it, but more customarily a special board was used as Shakespeare indicated. This would be about eighteen inches wide and three or four feet long divided into nine equal partitions latitudinally, each just the size of the coin used. Four or six coins would be used by each player in turn, the object being to slide them along the board so as to fill each partition in turn. A coin resting on a line would not count. At one time it was played with silver groats, hence its old name. Then Edward VI shillings were used, finally by the turn of the 19th century halfpennies, whence its modern name of shove-halfpenny.

Another game which contributed to the passing of Shovel-board was billiards. This seems to have originated in England or France around the start of the 17th century, but little appears to be known of it until Cotton mentioned it in his *Compleat Gamester* in 1674. He described the table as oblong with six pockets in the same form as the present table. Cues were termed masts and were tipped with ivory so that no spin could be applied. The balls themselves were usually of ivory, but quite often of wood and the bed of the table itself was oak covered with a fine green cloth. The cushions were stuffed with flox or cotton. A port, or small ivory arch, was placed where the end spot is now found and a small ivory peg, termed the king, placed on the centre spot at the baulk end. The object was to pass through the port, then touch the king with your opponent's ball, not your own, without knocking it over. Breaking the king resulted in a fine of one shilling. Breaking the port meant a fine of ten shillings. Clearly the finer points of the game had not then been developed, but Cotton thought it a 'gentile, cleanly and most ingenious game'.

The use of slate beds, and a tip on the cue, then finally rubber in the cushions about 1835 completely altered the game for the better. It began at once to be more popular and throughout the 19th century billiard saloons were being added on to public houses as the game became increasingly more fashionable and more scientific. The use of side and spin on the balls and the accuracy required by good players led to it becoming one of the most popular games of its kind. Numerous variations such as snooker and other lesser games merely added to its popularity. Like shovel-board, its only disadvantage was the amount of room it required and this in the end proved the limiting factor in its development, Although smaller tables were produced they were never as popular as the full-sized versions.

A seeming variant on billiards in much smaller form with a semi-circular top to the table and numbered ivory cups, sometimes known as Bar Billiards, or 'The Rocks of Sicily' is really a form of bagatelle and hence of considerably older origin. The earliest form of bagatelle seems to have been rolling balls on the flat, or down gentle slopes, through hoops or into holes with numbers of different value placed upon them. The size of the balls might vary from that of a marble upwards and this form of the game is said to owe its origins to idle choir boys or clerics amusing themselves in church pews during dull services. By the 6th century this had developed into a game known as 'Troul in Madame'. An explanation of this game dated 1572 runs as follows:

'The Ladys, Gentle Women, Wyves and Maydes . . . may have in the end of a Bench eleven holes made, into the which to trowle (i.e. roll) . . . bowles of lead, bigg, little, or mean, or also of Copper, Tynn, Wood, either vyolent or soft, after their own discretion, the pastyme Troule in Madame is termed . . .'

Gradually tables evolved with pins and similar obstacles in the way of the balls. Some were played on a slope either upwards or downwards and others on the flat. From this the 19th century game of bagatelle finally emerged in a number of contrasting forms. One of the variants, still found today, as noted above, was Bar Billiards. The most obvious, of course, is the modern pin table in its many forms, which, like the game of Hazard, crossed the Atlantic and returned in different form but still recognisable as a game with a history dating back more than four hundred years.

One common indoor sport, much patronised in inns, taverns and alehouses, which did not survive the 19th century, was cock-fighting. Supposedly popular with the Romans, it does not seem to have been to any degree popular in this country until the reign of Edward III, when it was listed as one of the sports prohibited in 1366. Nevertheless by the time Henry VIII had attained the throne it was once again popular and he had a cockpit constructed for his amusement at Whitehall. James I was also a keen cockfight supporter.

In 1614 Gervase Markham wrote a tract on: 'The Choice, Ordering, Breeding and Dyeting of the Fighting-Cocke for Battell' and stated: 'There is no pleasure more noble, delightsome, or void of cosenage and deceipt than the pleasure of Cockynge.' No doubt Gervase Markham wished to make the most of his subject, but certainly every indication is that exactly the opposite was the case and that few sports were more subject to different forms of cheating.

Charles Cotton in 1675 also spoke highly of cocking and his advice on the care of cocks before a fight was precise and detailed. He advised:

'Towards four or five o'clock in the evening . . . having lick't their eyes and head with your tongue, put them in their pens and having filled their troughs with square-cut manchet (white bread), piss therein and let them feed while the urine is hot; for this will cause the scouring to work, and will wonderfully cleanse both head and body.'

For a description of the scene at a cock-fight we can turn to Pepys. On 21st September, 1663 he wrote:

'I did go to Shoe Lane to see a cocke-fighting at a new pit there, a sport I was never at in my life; but Lord! to see the strange variety of people, from Parliament man (by name Wildes, that was Deputy Governor of the Tower . . .) to the poorest 'prentices, bakers, brewers, butchers, draymen and what not; and all these fellows one with another in swearing, cursing and betting. I soon had enough of it, and yet I would not but have seen it once, it being strange to observe the nature of these poor creatures, how they will fight till they drop dead upon the table and strike after they are ready to give up the ghost, not offering to run away when they are weary or wounded past doing further, whereas where a dunghill brood comes he will, after a sharp stroke that pricks him, run off the stage, and then they wring his neck without more ado, whereas the other they preserve, though their eyes be both out, for they breed only of a true cock of the game. Sometimes a cock that has had ten to one against him will by chance give an unlucky blow and will strike the other stark dead in a moment, that he never stirs more; but the common rule is that though a cock neither runs nor dies, yet if a man will bet twenty pounds to a crown and nobody takes the bet, the game is given over and not sooner. One thing more it is strange to see how people of this poor rank, that look as if they had not bread to put in their mouths, shall bet three or four pounds at one bet and lose it, and yet bet as much the next battle (so they call every match of two cocks) so that one of them will lose ten or twenty pounds at a meeting. Thence, having enough of it . . .'

A typical advertisement published in 1725 invited patrons of the Bell Inn at Norwich to attend a great cock match 'to show thirty-one cocks on a side for two guineas a cock and twenty guineas the odd battle . . . Gentlemen shall be accomodated with a glass of excellent wine and care taken to prevent disturbance by the mob.' The result, no doubt, was just such a scene as Pepys had witnessed.

Although declared illegal in 1849 cock-fighting was undoubtedly carried on clandestinely in some places until the end of the 19th century.

A notable example of an inn where cock-fighting was carried on until long after it had been declared illegal is the Garland Ox at Yarm in Yorkshire. There the sport had always been held in a cockpit in an upstairs attic. The inn itself is built in two halves so that when cock-fighting was declared illegal the solution was comparatively simple. The meetings were thereafter held in the attic adjacent to the one where they had been previously. The entrance to this was concealed behind a cupboard and access was only by the back stairs on the other side of the house. Thus, whenever the inn was raided by the policeman who suspected a meeting was being held, the participants would all slip down one set of back stairs while he was being escorted up to inspect the old cockpit by the other set of stairs. On the policeman's return they would all be found drinking innocently in a downstairs bar. The cocks themselves were disposed of in a weighted sack, which was dropped down an unused chimney flue that came out in a convenient outhouse. Whether they were ever caught in the act, or when the last match was held is not recorded.

Cock-fighting, of course, was always more popular in some districts than others and it survived longest in those localities in the north and west of England where it had enjoyed strong support. There are many inn games, or alehouse customs, which are likewise strongly local. Indeed, some games, though of similar origin to each other, have quite different characteristics in different localities.

A good example of the way in which games with similar origins have developed with entirely different local characteristics is that of skittles and nine-pins. Both derived without much doubt from the games of Kayles played in the 14th century and probably earlier. Basically this consisted of knocking down nine kayle-pins with a stick, or truncheon, thrown at them from a distance. At that time it was principally played outdoors.

In the West Country, especially, the game of Cloish, or Closh, was developed from Kayles. In this a bowl was used instead of a truncheon and was rolled along the ground instead of being hurled through the air. From this, in course of time, the game of nine-pin bowling developed with special indoor alleys, down which the bowls were rolled at the nine-pins.

In the home counties and adjacent areas on the other hand the kayle-pins came to be called kettle, or kittle, pins and so by easy stages skittles. Although a narrow cheese-shaped bowl was substituted for the truncheon the bowl was still thrown directly at the nine skittles. This too was brought indoors.

Thus two entirely different games with quite different rules were developed. In each case local rules and variations were sometimes quite marked from one area to the next. Derivations of each such as Dutch-pins, Four-corners and Rolly-polly, the latter played with a heavily biased bowl which was cast so as to use the bias and approach the pins from behind, were popular in some parts. By 1900 most of these variants had fallen out of use and only the two principal games remained entrenched in their respective areas.

At some period, probably during the 18th century, a table version of skittles was developed, once again principally in the home counties or adjacent areas, which was named for no obvious reason 'Devil Among The Tailors'. In this, a miniature set of nine skittles were thrown at with a ball tethered to a mast at one side of the board. In order to achieve success a considerable degree of practise had to be obtained as choosing the correct angle for releasing the tethered ball was all important. This, again, was an extremely localised game, only found, even in 1900, in a few inns or alehouses in certain areas.

Another very localised simple alehouse game, quite possibly of very ancient origins, was known as 'Ring the Bull'. A plain bull ring of metal, used for leading a bull by the nose, was hung from the ceiling by a cord. The object of the game was merely to swing the ring so as to ring a pin projecting from the wall. Although this sounds easy, like 'Devil Among The Tailors' it required considerable practice. By 1900 this too was only found in a few alehouses in country areas.

Darts and indoor quoits, each using a board on the wall, though now common and already well known by 1900, both seem to have been of comparatively recent origin. Darts was apparently known in the 17th century when a prisoner in the Bastille is recorded as having amused himself and whiled away the time by converting some long pins into darts which he threw at the wooden panels of his cell. Whether keen archers had earlier been in the habit of casting their arrows by hand against the panelling of their alehouse is another matter. The true origins of the game seem to be lost in the mists of alehouse smoke.

Another game which it has been claimed was invented by a prisoner in the Bastille is, of course, Solitaire. At the turn of the 19th century this game was not uncommon in the bars of some inns and alehouses for the benefit of unaccompanied customers. Played with pegs in holes, or marbles in hollows on a wooden base, the object was to take the forty-nine adjacent pegs by leap-frogging from one to the next, leaving finally one only remaining in the centre of the board.

It is doubtful whether the claims that marbles were played in inns or alehouses are in fact justified. However, Byng noted the side-effects of marbles on an inn he visited in Rotherham in 1789:

'Went to what is call'd the best inn, the Crown, but a more dreary, blacker, tumble-down, old casemented ruin, cou'd not be . . . and everything number'd for sale, if purchasers can be found; for the master of the inn has got a patent (a very odd one) for making marbles for children, which he can do, of all descriptions, so well and expeditiously, that he will soon supply all the schoolboys of the world.'

Of course, as has been pointed out, from the earliest days people have been accustomed to make their own amusements. Thus in country areas in the 18th and 19th centuries such simple amusements as pulling faces, or 'grinning matches' with each contestant thrusting his or her head through a horse collar were common. Similar amusements such as whistling matches, each trying to whistle while the others tried to put them off, or outwhistle them, or smoking matches, when a given amount of tobacco was smoked as fast or as slowly as possible, even yawning matches were all features of the country alehouse, or gathering.

In 1792 Byng noted on a journey near Stratford on Avon:

'Here were a crowd assembled, the remains of yesterday's wake, and two fellows upon stools, grinning for a wager (a sport I thought disused) so happily described in *The Spectator* – "The frightfullest grinner to be the winner." '

Such strange indoor sports as racing ferrets down the bar, or tortoises along a table, were always likely to be found in alehouses in the country and still are. Wagers on ducks, hens, geese and other animals have always been liable to crop up in conversation and, if possible, decided on the spot. Also from time immemorial there have been simple games played between customers in the inn, tavern or alehouse. As usual Pepys provides a good instance in his diaries:

'4th February 1661 . . . and I to the taverne where S. Wm Penn and the Comptroller and several others, men and women; and we had a very great and merry dinner. And after the Comptroller begun some sports; among others the Nameing of people round, and afterwards demanding Questions of them that they are forced to answer their names to; which doth make very good sport. And I took pleasure to take the forfeits of the ladies who could not do their duty, by kissing them . . .'

Finally, it must not be forgotten that one of the oldest indoor entertainments of the inn has for centuries been the acting of plays by touring groups of actors. In 1792 on a tour to the north Byng included the play bill of such a group, describing the scene as follows:

'Tuesday May 29th: . . . Huntingdon . . . The rain falling very hard I enter'd in haste the first inn, The Crown, a bad one it is, for no fire lighted and the stable is most dismal. There are players here, who perform tonight; and with a companion I might have been eag'r to have stay'd the play . . . FOR THE BENEFIT OF MR & MRS MILLER At the Theatre in the Crown Yard, HUNTINGDON, on Tuesday Evening May 29th, 1792, will be presented The Favorite Comedy (now performing at Covent Garden with universal Applause) called: THE ROAD TO RUIN.'

Chapter Ten

The Outdoor Sports

Bull- and Bear-Baiting – Pepys – Evelyn – Throwing at Cocks – Steele – Duck-pond – Strutt – Badger Baiting – Byng – Yattendon Revels – Maypoles – Bowls – Cotton – Quoits – Fives – Cricket – Knur & Spell – Prize fighting – Falconry – Coursing – Hunting – Fishing – Shooting – Coaching

At each inn on the road I a welcome could find:
At the Fleece I'd my skinfull of ale:
The Two Jolly Brewers were just to my mind:
At the Dolphin I drank like a Whale.
Tom Tun at the Hogshead sold pretty good stuff;
They'd capital flip at the Boar;
And when at the Angel I'd tippled enough,
I went to the Devil for more.

The Mail Coach Guard: ANON: 18th century.

THE OUTSIDE SPORTS associated with the alehouse, inn and tavern depended to a very large extent on its position, its surroundings, and the part of the country in which it was situated. Thus, for instance, certain inns were associated with bull-baiting in those parts of the country where that erstwhile so-called sport flourished. It is said that the ring to which the bull was tethered can still be seen in some places. After the event no doubt the enthusiastic supporters withdrew to the inn or alehouse to settle their wagers and discuss the performances of their dogs and plans for the future.

The history of bull- and bear-baiting with dogs goes back to the 12th century or earlier in England. The bull was tethered by a rope about fifteen feet long fastened round the base of its horns to a ring fixed in a stone embedded in the ground. The dogs were then urged on to attack it, with the object of seizing it by the nose and pinning its head securely to the ground. Bulldogs and mastiffs, particularly the breed known eventually as the Staffordshire bull-terrier, were bred and trained principally for this purpose and for dog fighting matches.

Pepys on 14th August, 1666 wrote of a visit he and his wife paid to the Bear Garden in London:

'I have not been, I think, of many years and saw some good sport of the bull's tossing of the dogs; one into the very boxes. But it is a very rude and nasty pleasure . . '

Evelyn wrote in his diary on June 16th, 1670:

'I went with some friends to the Bear Garden, where was cock-fighting, dog fighting and bear and bull baiting, it being a famous day for all these butcherly sports . . . The bulls did exceedingly well, but the Irish wolf-hound exceeded, which was a tall greyhound, a stately creature indeed, who beat a cruel mastiff. One of the bulls tossed a dog full into a lady's lap as she sate in one of the boxes at a considerable height from the arena. Two poor dogs were killed . . .'

He had previously recorded a more unpleasant scene in August 1667:

'There was now a very gallant horse baited to death with dogs; but he fought them all, so as the fiercest of them could not fasten on him, till the men ran him through with their swords. This wicked and barbarous sport deserved to have been punished in the cruel contrivers to get money under the pretence that the horse had killed a man, which was false. I would not be persuaded to be a spectator.'

Another common sport, which had as ancient origins and was still popular in the 17th century, was throwing at cocks. The cock would be tethered to a post and cudgels thrown at it until the wretched bird was killed. Alternatively, in a slightly more humane form, it was enclosed in an earthenware pot specially made for the purpose, with its head and tail exposed. This was then hung some fourteen feet from the ground and the cudgel thrower who shattered the pot gained the bird as his prize.

As early as 1709 Sir Richard Steele writing on this subject noted:

'Some French writers have represented this diversion of the common people much to our disadvantage, and imputed it to a natural fierceness and cruelty of temper, as they do some other entertainments peculiar to our nation; I mean those elegant diversions of bull-baiting and prize-fighting, with the like ingenious diversions of the bear garden. I wish I knew how to answer this reproach which is cast upon us and excuse the death of so many innocent cocks, bulls, dogs and bears as have been set together by the ears, or died an untimely death only to give us sport.'

Another so-called sport frequently practised in neighbourhoods where a duck pond adjoined an inn or alehouse was to release a pinioned duck on the pond and match various dogs in attempts to retrieve it. When the dog swam close enough, of course, the duck dived, but was unable to take to flight. Eventually one dog would retrieve it and the owner would win the wager and the duck. Meanwhile the inn or alehouse keeper would have greatly enhanced his custom.

Such sports were still common late in the 18th century since Strutt mentions the case in 1760 of an owl being concealed in a pot, such as those mentioned as used for throwing at cocks. The head and tail of a cock were then exposed to view and the pot hung in position. The yokel who broke the pot with his cudgel was astonished to see the owl, thus liberated, fly off, leaving him with the broken pot and the head and tail of the cock he had expected.

By 1800 most of these cruel sports had lapsed naturally, except in very rural and backward areas. Yet two attempts to introduce a bill to declare bull-baiting illegal in 1802 and 1829 were both defeated. It was not until 1835 that bull-baiting was finally declared illegal. Even then isolated cases of bull-baitings were reported until as late as 1853.

Badger-baiting was another of these so-called sports, which survived long after bull-baiting had been declared illegal. The wretched badger, by nature a nocturnal animal, with extremely powerful jaws, was dug out of his earth and placed in a barrel. There, he naturally retreated into the darkest corner. The dogs of the neighbourhood were then urged on to 'draw' him from his shelter. It was only around the turn of the 19th century that this cruel practice finally lapsed, although isolated instances may have occurred in the early 1900s.

Of course it is easy today to forget that in the 17th and 18th centuries

Grinning through a horse collar ; 1836

A dancing bear outside The Old King of Bohemia

there was an entirely different attitude to life. Anaesthetics did not exist, infant mortality was high and only the hardy survived. Pepys described prize-fights where swords 'little if at all blunter on the edge than the common swords are' were used and the contestants were 'all over blood.' Although such exhibitions had died out by the mid-18th century the bare-fisted pugilism which took its place was little, if at all, better. Nor were many country sports, such a cudgel-fighting, any great improvement.

As late as 1795 on a ride round Oxfordshire, Byng quoted an advertisement he found in a newspaper, recording with evident relish:

'I am ever greedy when travelling to read the country papers . . . and I was glad to find by this advertisement, that neither manhood or gaiety have yet foresaken the country . . .:

YATTENDON REVEL

'This is to give Notice that Yattendon Revel will be kept as usual on Monday the 11th of July instant, and for the encouragement of Gentlemen, gamesters and others, there will be given a Good Gold-laced Hat, of 27s value, to be played for at Cudgels; the man that breaks the most heads to have the prize; 2s will be given to each man that positively breaks a head, for the first ten heads that are broke; and 1s to the man that has his head broke; but the man is not to receive the 2s unless he gets up and plays the ties off; the blood to run an inch or be deemed no head. The ties to be played out to prevent any number of gamesters from sharing the prize, unless by the umpires consent, whose decision shall be final; no person shall be allowed to give a head, but if the umpires should object to any person he will be allowed 2s 6d.

'Also will be given a Silver-laced Hat, to be Wrestled for; the man that throws most men to have the prize; no dispute about falls, but three go-downs.

'Likewise, an exceedingly good Gold-laced Hat, of 27s value, to be bowled for; 3d three bowls; the man that gets the most pins at three bowls to have the prize. To begin bowling at one o'clock and end at nine.

'The umpires will positively be on the stage at three o'clock precisely.

'THE SECOND REVEL DAY. July the 12th. Will be given, Half-a-Guinea to be run for by Jack Asses. The best of three heats. No less than three will be allowed to start.

'Also will be given a fine Holland Smock to be run for by women; the best of three heats. No less than three will be allowed to start.

'Also a Gold-Laced Hat of 27s value, to be played at Cudgels for. The man that wins the hat on the first day will not be permitted to play for this – the same rules to be observed as the first day.

'Likewise tobacco to be grinn'd for, by old women, through a horse collar as usual.

'And an exceedingly good Gold-Laced Hat of 27s value to be bowled for; – the same rules to be observed as on the first day: the Sport to begin precisely at three o'clock.

'Stalls for people to put their goods on to be had at The Royal Oak, as usual.'

From a similar programme for Rustic Sports in East Anglia dated 1812 there were such competitions as: 'A pig hunt by eight men; One pound of tobacco to be smoked for by 6 men; A race by females for a handsome gown-piece. Married Ladies will be allowed to contest for this prize by having their husband's consent . . . Single Ladies to wear DRAWERS.' No doubt, once again, the local inn or alehouse keeper was one of the principal organisers and benefited considerably as a result.

Naturally the inn and alehouse keepers encouraged any games on the village greens, or on land (or duckponds) adjoining their own premises, which were likely to be good for custom. Thus on the Restoration there were even spasmodic attempts to revive dancing round the maypole. Pepys recorded in his diaries:

'May 1st 1660: This morning I was told how the people of Deale have set up two or three Maypoles and have hung up their flags upon the top of them and do resolve to be very merry today . . .'

As late as 13th June, 1789 Byng recorded in a tour of the Midlands in Derbyshire:

'Rode thro' Normanton, a village, where a May Pole was, as others of this country, richly adorn'd by garlands composed of silk, gauze and mock flowers; and around which (a woman told me) they danced in the Morris way; but not in honour of the goddess Maia on the 1st of her month, but rather in memory of the Restoration upon the 29th of May.'

The Puritans had left their impress on the countryside too thoroughly for such revivals to be very widespread. Nor were such occasions frequent enough for the inn or alehouse keepers to benefit greatly by them. They concentrated rather on encouraging entertainment and games which could be conducted outside throughout the greater part of the year, or at least during the summer months when the longer light allowed their customers greater leisure time out of doors.

One such game which proved good for custom was bowls. When this originated is uncertain, but the first known illustration of the game appears in a manuscript of the 13th century. At this time the object seems to have been to bowl to a mark, or cone, set upright at some distance from the bowler. During the ensuing centuries the small bowl, or jack, used as a mark near to which the bowls had to be rolled seems to have been introduced and the game developed very much on modern lines.

Pepys entered in his diary:

'May 1st 1661: Up early and baited (i.e. rested) at Petersfield in the room which the king lay in lately at his being there. Here very merry and played with our wives at bowles . . .'

In his *Compleat Gamester* in 1675 Charles Cotton viewed bowls with some disfavour because of the amount of gambling on the game which was apparently involved at that time. He wrote:

'A Bowling-green or Bowling-alley is a place where three things are thrown away besides the Bowls; viz, Time, Money and Curses, and the last ten for one. The best sport in it is the Gamesters, and he enjoys it that looks on and bets nothing. It is a School of Wrangling . . . for here men will wrangle for a hair's breadth . . .'

A bowling alley at this time did not necessarily mean a covered alley, but merely a narrow lawn between pathways, or hedges. Since many of the greens were very rough indeed accuracy must have been difficult in the extreme. The lawns then were of course close cut with a scythe and rolled with a stone roller, but even so they were scarcely up to modern standards. The bowls used were either the ordinary round bowl without a bias, or cheese-shaped biased bowls, which required considerable skill and practise to use with any degree of accuracy. In either case the game seems often to have been used as an excuse for heavy drinking as well as betting. In a tour of the Midlands in 1789 Byng noted near Ashbourne:

'In a summer house of a bowling green, the neighbouring squires were assembled in noisy mirth (hard to determine whether merry or quarrelling). I remark'd that the truest derivation of *Bowling*-Green was from the number of *Bowls* of Punch or negus (i.e. hot wine punch) drunk thereon.'

Byng was an acute observer of rural customs and he also noted in his tour of the Midlands in 1789:

'At Duckmanton were some young fellows playing at quoits, a game much in vogue hereabouts; of the weight of the quoits and the length of the cast, I ask'd particulars of a remarkably fine young fellow, whom I eyed with the looks of a recruiting officer; and he answered that the former weigh'd 10 lbs and that the cast was 25 yards.'

There can be very little doubt that quoits originated with the throwing of horseshoes at an iron pin stuck firmly in the ground and indeed this sport is still carried on in some parts of the U.S.A. and in France. By the 15th century it had developed into a more organised sport, when an iron quoit weighing a pound was used. There is a reference to a child being struck on the head with such a quoit in 1409 and being given up for dead, but recovering miraculously, to the great relief of the carpenter, one Richard Wodewell, who had overthrown the mark extremely carelessly by twelve feet. Clearly, despite being amongst the numerous sports prohibited by law in favour of archery, quoits was frequently played.

In principle, an iron pin, usually called a hob, about eighteen inches long was fixed into the ground within a few inches of its top and at a distance of anything between ten and twenty-five yards another pin was inserted. The quoits which might be from one pound up to eleven pounds in weight were then thrown alternately by two equally matched teams of up to four a side. By 1900 the game was still being played in much the same form but with very considerable local variations as to marking methods and the form of play as well as the weight of quoits and length of pitch. There is no doubt that the game still had a peculiar spell on the participants.

Yet another game which Byng noted being played was fives. During his tour in North Wales in 1792, he observed: 'Oswestry; Here the taste for fives playing begins to shew itself, with which men and boys batter the church walls . . .' From the 14th century onwards it was the custom in many parts of the country, although notably in the west, to play fives with a ball against the church walls. Usually the north wall was chosen since this was customarily free from graves and less likely to cause indignation or criticism.

In the West Country the sport took such a hold that many inns erected their own fives walls, against which their customers could play. Although fives playing itself has long ceased to be a sport likely to be encountered in the grounds of an inn or alehouse some of these fives walls are still to be found. As late as the 18th and 19th centuries it seems that tournaments were sometimes organised against neighbouring villages in the West Country and the game had many dedicated supporters.

Perhaps one of the commonest games conducted on the village green with which the inn has always been closely associated was village cricket. Its exact origins are obscure, but probably similar to those of stoolball, still played in Sussex and thought to have originated from milkmaids throwing stones at a milking stool. The oldest known reference to cricket appears to be towards the end of the 16th century. It was certainly played throughout most of the 17th century and became extremely popular in the 18th century. It was particularly keenly played in Kent and Hampshire and Hambledon in Hampshire claims to be the birthplace of cricket.

The rules for the game were drawn up formally in the year 1774 by a committee of noblemen and gentlemen who met at The Star and Garter Inn in Pall Mall. Notwithstanding this, there seem to have been many local variations on the rules at that time. There were even some rather startling attempts to change the nature of the game entirely, though not without benefit to the innkeeper, as may be noted from an advertisement in the Kentish Gazette of 29th April, 1794:

'Cricketing on horseback – A singular game of cricket will be played on Tuesday the 6th of May in Linsted Park between the Gentlemen of the Hill and the Gentlemen of the Dale, for one guinea a man. The whole to be performed on horseback. To begin at nine o'clock and to be played out. A good ordinary on the ground by John Hogben.'

Throughout the 19th century village cricket was amongst the most popular and widespread of sports. Inter-village rivalry was high and inter-county cricket was followed with immense enthusiasm. All this was good for the inn and the alehouse keepers, who no doubt did their best to encourage it. By the turn of the century it was still firmly established in the Victorian mind as the most characteristically English of games.

Less characteristic, indeed essentially a game played in certain areas in northern England only (although possibly stemming from similar origins to cricket and a game called Bat and Trap recently revived in Kent) was a rather strange game called Knur and Spell which was played with a mallet and a small ball known as the knur made of hard china, or staghorn weighted with lead. The trap, or spell, was a spring-loaded device which released the ball to a predetermined height in the air, when it was struck with the mallet. The object was to see how far the ball could be struck. Distances of over 300 yards were sometimes achieved. Although an apparently simple, even pointless game, this enjoyed considerable popularity in the north of England with considerable sums wagered on local champions, but by the 1900s it was already on the wane.

As already noted and as is clear from the localised nature of many of these outdoor and indoor sports, the question of whether they were popular, or even known, depended entirely on the geographical position of the inn or alehouse. Apart from that, its actual position in a village, or in the country, whether near a village green, or a mill stream, or at a convenient crossroads suitable for the meet of a pack of hounds, was always another factor which had to be taken into account. These were points particularly affecting inns with regard to the sports of the countryside, hunting, shooting, fishing, coursing and racing. Only where it was convenient for their purposes were such sportsmen likely to patronise an inn or alehouse.

During the late 18th and early 19th centuries the position of an inn could be of great importance when the organisers of a bare-fist prize-fight were considering whether to choose it as their headquarters. Since such matches were officially illegal it often happened that a zealous magistrate would appear on the scene of such an encounter and insist on the participants and spectators moving out of his area of jurisdiction. Yet as soon as they moved into a neighbouring county where the magistrates did not uphold the law so firmly he might relax his scruples sufficiently to watch the match with interest himself. Such ambivalent attitudes to the law were not uncommon and whenever possible the organisers of such matches chose as their headquarters inns close to at least two county boundaries.

It followed therefore that inns such as the Bull at Barton Mills, close to the unenclosed breck lands of Norfolk at nearby Elvedon, were patronised in the 18th century by falconers. When Colonel Thomas Thornton founded the Falconer's Club of Great Britain in 1772 it was there they used to meet. When he handed over his hawks to the President of the Club, the Earl of Orford, in 1781, he was presented with a silver gilt trophy of a goshawk holding a hare inscribed:

'Colonel Thornton . . . is requested to receive this piece of plate from George, Earl of Orford together with the united thanks of the members of the Falconer's Club . . . Barton Mills. 23rd June 1781.'

Similarly the Rutland Arms in Newmarket was associated with much early horse racing. It was there that Osbaldestone, Squire of All England as he was known, won his classic wager of a thousand guineas by riding two hundred miles in less than ten hours. He performed the feat in eight hours forty-two minutes and then had a good dinner and spent most of the night playing billiards. It was in the same inn that the second coursing society in England, the Newmarket Coursing Society, was formed in 1806 and thereafter met regularly. Later on, in 1830, the Waterloo Cup, the premier prize in coursing, was to be presented by the proprietor of the Waterloo Inn in Liverpool. The associations of inns with sport is endless.

Byng knew what he was talking about on the subject of inns and he was keen on hunting and fishing. In his tour to North Wales in 1784 he wrote:

'North Leach is a poor dismal place, built of stone that turns black; and gives a very monastic look; and yet (cou'd I afford it) how I should like to pass a November in such a place and country with a sociable hunting, whist party, and our own wine! To hold a good horse in my hand every morning; then a good glass of wine; and then a good quantity of trumps . . .'

In his tour to the north in 1792 he wrote in contrasting vein:

'Malham: Now I might like a fishing party; several parties come here for the grouse shooting (these are the pursuits of the country); but when I intended such a scheme, I should send beforehand, to secure rooms, and stabling; my servant would see they were properly fitted up; the windows well glazed, the doors to shut tight, the grate repaired; and when I came, think you that I would lay in their beds and drink their poisons? No, no; my bed and bedding, my hampers of wine, my books, my backgammon table should be ready to receive me.'

During a tour in Lincolnshire in 1791 he noted: at Folkingham:

'My landlord said that any gentlemen coming to his inn at the season may shoot with Sir H.G.'s gamekeeper and that partridges are plenty.' He had earlier assessed the costs of a friend's shooting as follows: 'C. came in from his last day's sport with another leash of birds, making in all four brace and a half; all shot by H. for C. C. has never touched a feather! Nor could I now conceal a sarcastic laughter after all the expense that C. put himself to for shooting apparatus; for everything but the most necessary and first to be thought of article, a gun; and to my calculations of his costs, he pleaded guilty: Exactly one guinea a brace!

Game Certificate	£2	3s
Patent Shot		8
Powder		4
Flask		8
Gaiters		5
Shot Bag		3
Flints		1
Horse hire to Potton		12
To Mr. H.		10
	4	14 0'

On a tour to the Midlands in 1799 while staying at The Haycock at Wansford he pictured his favourite sports and the favoured position of the inn.

'After breakfast to my usual sports, lunging my horse, and to fishing, where, ignorant of the right haunts, and tackling, I caught but seven fish, one a bream of a pound, which was ordered for dinner. After dinner at five o'clock, I realised my hopes about fishing; by catching some very fine chubs and bream, several that made my small rod to crack . . . to my right, at a distance, a mill; to my left, Wansford Bridge, and village; and behind me the London road descends a gradual hill, where I can see every passing carriage.'

Certain sports, although they gained general acceptance and even considerable popularity, were never, for one reason or another, closely associated with inns, taverns or alehouses. Amongst these were Pele Mell, a forerunner of croquet, football, archery, polo and golf. True the participants might adjourn to inns or alehouses afterwards and some inns may have introduced croquet lawns or archery butts, or even clock golf and putting greens, but these hardly constitute inn sports in the sense of the others considered already.

With the decline of the coaching services following the spread of the railway it is perhaps not surprising that coaching became a recognised sport in itself. Some idea of the sort of pleasure to be had from a coach journey is provided by Colonel Peter Hawker's description in his Diary of a stage-coach journey to Exeter in 1811:

'We were a delightfully jolly party, and it not being a post-day, the mail stopped whenever we saw game, and during the journey I killed four brace of partridges. When it was too dark to shoot, our party mounted the roof and sang choruses (which I joined in and drove) and in which the guard and coachman took a very able part.'

During the latter half of the 19th century several clubs such as 'The Four in Hand' and others of a like nature were formed by enthusiasts who maintained their own coaches and arranged regular coaching meetings. With the roads almost deserted, it must have been a splendid sensation and a welcome must have been assured at every erstwhile coaching inn on their chosen routes. Although some of these coaches were still being maintained as late as the Edwardian era, the advent of the motor-car finally spelled the end for them, while paradoxically bringing a new lease of life to the inns that had served them.

Chapter Eleven

The Highland Inn

Auld Alliance – Usquebaugh – Highlands and Lowlands – Lack of Inns, 1617 – John Taylor – Braemar – Dunbar – Cockburnspath – Captain Burt – Effects of Culloden – Colonel Thornton – Luss – Killin – Dalnacardoch – Dalmally – Kelso – Keswick – Mrs. M'Kenzie of Tomintoul – Whisky drinking in 18th century – Illicit Stills – St. John's description of one – Highland Sports – Highland Sporting Inn

Wha' first shall rise to gang awa',
A cuckold, coward, loon is he!
Wha' last beside his chair shall fa',
He is the king amang us three!
We are na fou, we're nae that fou,
But just a drappie in our e'e:
The cock may craw, the day may draw,
And ay we'll taste the barley bree. (whisky)

From 'Willie brew'd a peck o' maut': ROBERT BURNS: 1789.

IT IS EASY to forget that Scotland and England were separate and often warring nations until the final Union of 1707. Previous to that the 'auld alliance' between Scotland and France against England had served to separate the countries not only in war, but also in peace. It is no accident that many of the Scots Lowland towns more closely resemble their French rather than their English counterparts. Nor is it surprising that throughout the 17th and for much of the 18th centuries the educated Scots palates were more attuned to claret and the wines of France than their English equivalents. While the English drank beer and gin, the Scots drank ale and wine, and from the 17th century onwards increasing quantities of whisky.

Prior to the 18th century the Scots seldom drank beer and even today the Scots beer is noticeably sweeter than the English. Strong ale was certainly drunk in considerable quantities, but from the 17th century onwards 'Usquebaugh', Gaelic for 'The Water of Life', soon shortened to 'Usque' and thence to whisky, was increasingly the national drink. The actual origins of whisky are shrouded in Highland mists of the past, but it seems probable that it was introduced in the late 15th century and became gradually more common throughout the 17th century before finally attaining the status of a national drink in the 18th century, both in the Highlands and Lowlands.

To understand the development of the Highland Inn it is necessary to appreciate that the Highlands of Scotland, cut off by a barrier of mountains, by a separate language, clan system and distinctive dress and customs from the Lowlands and the Borders, were, to all intents and purposes, a foreign country until the 18th century. Prior to then, there were no inns in the Highlands since their standards of hospitality were such that no Highlander would turn a stranger from his door. Even as late as the 17th century, inns as they were understood in England, scarcely existed in the Lowlands either. Fynes Morison in his *Itinerary* written in 1617 noted:

'I did never see nor heare that they (the Scots) have any publike Innes with signes hanging out, but the better sort of Citizens brew Ale their usuall drinke (which will distemper a stranger's bodie) and the same Citizens will entertaine passengers upon aquaintance or entreaty.'

John Taylor, during his *Pennyless Pilgrimage* in 1618, found Scotland very much to his liking. At the start he wrote:

'The Scots do allow almost as large a measure of their miles as they do of their drink, for an English gallon either of ale or wine is but their quart and one Scottish mile now and then may well stand for a mile and a half or two English.'

Significantly he made no mention of inns in Edinburgh or further north and since he was never slow to praise or criticize whenever he stayed at one the likelihood is that he received private hospitality, thus bearing out Fynes Morison's comments. Be that as it may, he waxed enthusiastic on the subject of his entertainment in Edinburgh:

'In the High Stret, Edinburgh. There I find entertainment beyond expectations and there is fish, flesh, bread and fruit in such variety that I think I may offenceless call it superfluity or satiety. The worst was that wine and ale was so scarce and the people there such misers of it that every night before I went to bed, if any man had asked me a civil question, all the wit in my head could not have given him a sober answer.'

Ready for anything, as ever, he went on to the Highlands and went hunting with the Earl of Mar in the Braes of Mar, adopting the kilt for the purpose. The old Highland method of driving the deer into a glen surrounded with 'a hundred couple of strong Irish greyhounds' was employed and 'with dogs, guns, arrows, dirks and daggers in the space of two hours four score fat deer were slain'.

He mentioned sampling Usquebaugh, but made no mention of any Highland sports other than deer hunting. Since as far back as the 11th century it had been the custom for clan chiefs to keep a 'Manhood Stone', or Clad Cuid Fir, weighing over a hundredweight, which was usually kept near the entrance of their castle for visitors to demonstrate their strength. At Inver, near Braemar, such a stone weighing 268 lbs. is still to be seen, but Taylor made no mention of it. He went on instead to Brechin, where he experienced a different test of manhood:

'A wench . . . came into my chamber at midnight (I being asleep) and she opening the bed would fain have lodged with me . . . But I no sooner knew who it was, but I arose and thrust (her) . . . out of my chamber and for want of a lock or latch I staked up my door with a great chair . . . Had not this Highland Irish house helped me at a pinch I should have sworn that all Scotland had not been so kind as to have bestowed a louse upon me; but with a shift that I had, I shifted off my cannibals and was no more troubled with them.'

He finally left Scotland by way of Dunbar, where he enjoyed a last carousal in the High Street in a house owned by Mr. James Bailie, now the St. George Inn. Remembering his account of Scottish measures and even allowing for exaggeration he and his companions seem to have drunk a considerable amount. Notable also is the fact that it is wine, not ale, or whisky which was drunk at this time:

'Master John Acmootye, one of the Grooms of His Majesty's bed Chamber, and Master James Acmootye went to the town of Dunbar with me, where ten Scottish pints of wine were consumed and brought to nothing for a farewell. There at Master James Bailie's house I took leave and Master James Acmootye coming for England said If I would ride with him that neither I nor my horse should want betwixt that place and London . . .'

It was only after leaving Dunbar and approaching the Border on the main route north and south that John Taylor first mentioned an inn, as such, and the experience seems to have left even him fumbling for words at this final example of Scottish hospitality. Since no inn could possibly have functioned in the manner he described, it could be that he unwittingly stumbled on the headquarters of the free-traders, or more probably on one of their dispersal points. Cockburnspath, where he spent the night, is close to Eyemouth, well known as a smuggling centre and literally honeycombed with secret passages. Cove itself, the tiny local harbour, has a network of caves in the cliffs beside it, ideal for concealing any contraband. The landlord could well have had good reason for ensuring that his guests slept soundly. Taylor recorded:

'That night he (James Acmootye) brought me to a place called Cockburnspath, where we lodged at an inn the like of which, I daresay, is not in any of his Majesty's dominions. And for to show my thankfulness to Master William Arnot and his wife, the owners thereof, I must explain their bountiful entertainment of guests, which is this. Suppose ten, or fifteen, or twenty men and horses come to lodge at their house, the men shall have flesh, tame and wild fowl, fish, with all variety of good cheer, good lodging and welcome; and the horses shall want neither hay, nor good provender. This is the worthy gentleman's use, his chief delight being only to give strangers entertainment gratis.'

The same year as Taylor's journey, 1618, saw the start of the Thirty Years War on the Continent. Before its end the amount of whisky distilling had sufficiently increased for the Scottish Parliament to impose a tax on it in 1644. This was, rather surprisingly, reduced by 'Brewer' Cromwell, so named because of his mother's occupation, and lapsed entirely with the Restoration in 1660. Meanwhile the Scots mercenaries returned from the Continent had introduced the game of draughts, which became a popular pastime in the emerging Lowland Inns and 'howffs', or ale and spirit houses. The other principal Lowland pastimes were bowling, curling on the ice in winter, shinty, a fierce game resembling all-in hockey, and, of course, golf.

In 1693, under William III, the tax on whisky was re-introduced and with the Union of 1707 the Excise Gauger was also introduced into Scotland. There followed in 1713 a tax on malt. Although this was only at half the English level it was highly unpopular and resulted in an immediate increase in smuggling and evasion.

So far, few, if any, of these southern ideas, or taxes, had had much effect in the Highlands, still virtually impenetrable due to lack of roads. The idea that an inn was needed for travellers would have shocked the Highlander's principles of hospitality. From the chief to the simplest clansman the very thought of turning a traveller away from their door was anathema. It was only after the English had penetrated the Highlands following the abortive 1715 Rebellion that such ideas began to spread.

The earliest account of a Highland Inn is to be found in the letters of Captain Edward Burt, who was on General Wade's staff from 1724–1728 endeavouring to drive roads through the Highlands for the first time. This Engineer officer gives some interesting, if biased, pictures of the Highland scene. He described his arrival at a 'publick Hut', probably at Dalnacardoch, which served as an inn, as follows:

'The Landlord not only sits down with you, as in the northern Lowlands, but in some little time asks Leave (and sometimes not) to introduce his Brother, Cousin, or more, who are all to drink your Honour's Health in *Usky*, which tho' a strong Spirit, is to them like Water. And this I have often seen 'em drink out of a Scollop Shell.'

It is very clear that Captain Burt had no understanding of the Highland character, but in this he was not alone. The Lowland Scots also were unable to understand these 'barbarians' on their doorstep. By sanctioning wittingly, or unwittingly, the betrayal of hospitality which resulted in the notorious Massacre of Glencoe, William III, whose signature was on the order, made himself the most hated man in the Highlands and provided the basic mistrust of the government in the south which resulted in both the 1715 and 1745 Rebellions. Such Acts during his reign as those 'for rooting out the Erse language and for other *pious* uses' indicated a deep seated determination to eliminate not only the Gaelic but the Highland way of life.

Throughout the 18th century, after their final stand against an encroaching civilisation at Culloden, the Highlanders were systematically 'rooted out' of the Highlands. Forbidden to wear the kilt, their national dress, or carry arms as was their custom, those, who did not emigrate or join the British armed forces to fight and die for their erstwhile foe, were evicted from their homes to make way first for cattle and ultimately for sheep. Betrayed by their own chieftains the Highlanders and their way of life were doomed. During the entire 18th century and the first part of the 19th century the massive evictions continued. Finally, in many cases, the chieftains themselves were bought out and replaced by English absentee landlords as the old way of life crumbled before their eyes.

Those English visitors brave enough to penetrate the Highlands dur-the 18th century despite the stories of 'awesome' mountains and 'terrific' gorges were agreeably surprised. One of the first was that redoubtable Yorkshire sportsman Colonel Thomas Thornton, huntsman, falconer, fisherman and shooting man. Travelling in considerable style, with his carriage, servants, artist and dogs, as well as guns, rods and supplies of wine and porter, he toured the Highlands extensively in 1784. In his *Highland Tour* he wrote on Loch Lomond:

'Landed at the village of *Luss*, called here a *town*, which name they give even to four or five cabins . . . came to the inn . . . Great complaints were made by the servants . . . that the stables were not divided, the hay bad, but little straw and no coach-house . . . Our beds were, all things considered, very comfortable . . .

'. . . at Tarbat. It has always been a rule with me, to defer giving my opinion of an inn till I have examined the most useful part, I mean the *inside*. The rooms here were small indeed, but they were clean, and we wanted nothing more; better linen I never saw, and every attention was shown to us that the most finical traveller could have wished . . . We sat down to a plain but really neat board: I eat the whitings and the gentlemen did honour to the trout; our wine was tolerable, London porter delicious; and on visiting our beds, we found them very comfortable indeed.'

After an extremely bad inn at Crianlarich, he was agreeably surprised to find an old acquaintance of his in charge of the inn at Killin. He recorded:

'Killin; though the inn at Cree-in-la-Roche is bad, the traveller is here amply recompensed. I never saw a better inn than that at Killin; Lord Breadalbane, much to his credit, having taken great pains to make it very commodious. The landlord I found had been a neighbour of mine; a lively, honest Yorkshireman, who had frequently hunted with my hounds and knew me perfectly well, as did also his wife, a neat, active woman, who soon got us everything we could wish for . . .'

At Dalnacardoch, where Captain Burt had suffered in the 'publick Hut', he found himself extremely well looked after. He wrote:

'Dalnacardock . . . Liquors and provisions of all kinds at Dalnacardock were plentiful and excellent . . . finding our quarters so agreeable determined to stay here the evening . . . (they went out fishing and caught thirty trout and one char with ease) arrived about eight o'clock and found dinner just ready . . .

Hodge Podge
Pudding Greens
Trout and Char
Roast mutton, excellent
Second Course
Brandered Cickens
Cold Hams
Snipes
Cheshire Cheese-biscuits
Wines
Claret, good – port, ditto
Limes, Jamaica Rum and
Incomparable *porter* from *Calvert's*'

He went on to visit many parts of the Highlands, shooting, fishing and hawking as he went. He commented particularly favourably on the inns at Inverness and Dalmally; the latter as follows:

'Dalmally . . . heard the sound of music . . . a ball . . . in consequence of the harvest-home . . . They were dancing . . . the true Glen Orgue kick . . . it gave me great pleasure to see . . . with what spirit they danced. How much more rational . . . than . . . our labourers in England, who in their way would be intoxicated and riotous.'

Finally he returned south, incidentally giving a good picture of a Lowland Inn at Kelso, when the annual Kelso Races were in progress:

'The Highland Still' after Sir David Wilkie

Old Mab, the highwayman, stops Judge Jeffreys

'Kelso . . . Arrive at the inn. A charming scene of confusion; cooks, waiters, servants and ladies running against each other, being the . . . annual meeting at Kelso Races . . . Dinner was just ready and we had scarcely time to pull off our boots, which is indispensibly necessary, ladies dining at the ordinary . . .

'Oct. 22nd . . . Up by eight, and proceeded; found from the stupidity of the waiters, ringing of bells &c., that the party which had sat down when the ball broke up was still drinking and meant to sit till hounds went out . . .'

At last back in England in the Lake District, he found the standard of the inn there poor and recorded:

'Keswick; arrived at our inn, which we found inferior to most of the Highland Inns, a circumstance unpardonable in a country much more frequented . . .'

Thornton's *Tour* was not published until 1804 and although he claimed it was the diary of a journey made in 1784 it was really the product of a number of visits made in the 1780s. Even so he was well before his time. His was the advance party of that army of sporting tourists, who were to invade the Highlands annually from the mid-19th century onwards for the fishing, shooting and stalking and even for the scenery once Victoria and Albert had settled at Balmoral and by their example had made the Highlands 'respectable'.

Even in the late 18th century it was plain that the natural Highland hospitality and courtesy produced good inns. The landlords and landladies naturally wished to provide their guests with all that they desired. They were also clean as well as courteous. These traits were implicit in the Highland character. However no description of the Highland Inns at this period would be complete without the entertaining account of the remarkable landlady of the inn at Tomintoul, ably described in the Statistical Account of Scotland for 1790 by the Rev. Mr. John Grant:

'In personal respect and fortune at the head of the inhabitants (of Tomintoul) must be ranked Mrs M'Kenzie of the best inn at the sign of the horns. This heroine began her career of celebrity in the accomodating disposition of an easy virtue, at the age of fourteen in 1745. That year saw her in Flanders, caressing and caressed. Superior to the little prejudices of her sex she relinquished the first object of her affection and attached herself to a personage high in the military department. After a campaign or two spent in acquiring a knowledge of man and the world, Scotland saw her again; but wearied of the inactivity of rural retirement she then married and made her husband enlist in the Royal Highlanders at the commencement of the war in 1756. With him she navigated the Atlantic and sallied forth on American ground in quest of adventures, equally prepared to meet her friends, or encounter her enemies in the fields of Venus or Mars as occasion offered. At the conclusion of the war she revisited her native country. After a variety of vicissitudes in Germany, France, Holland, England, Ireland, Scotland, America and the West Indies her anchor is now moored on dry land in the village of Tamnetoul. It might be imagined that such extremes of climate, so many rugged paths, so many severe bruises, as she must have experienced in her progress through life would have impaired her health, especially when it is considered that she added twenty-four children to the aggregate of general births beside some homunculi which stopped short in their passage. Wonderful, however, as it may appear, at this moment she is as fit for her usual active life as ever; and except two or three grey hairs vegetating from a mole upon one of her cheeks, that formerly set off a high ruddy complexion, she still retains all the apparent freshness and vigour of youth.'

There is very little doubt that had she been asked to what she ascribed her surprising vigour Mrs. M'Kenzie would have replied succinctly and with no hesitation whatever: 'Whisky'. Throughout the 18th century whisky was drunk throughout the Highlands as Captain Burt had observed in 1724 'like water'. Elizabeth Grant of Rothiemurchus in her *Memoirs of a Highland Lady*, 1797–1827, recalled the enormous amount of whisky drinking common. Everyone was automatically offered whisky and even small children drank it. She recalled:

'Aunt Mary had a story that one day a woman with a child in her arms and another bit thing at her knee, came up among them; the horn cup was duly handed to her, she took a 'gey guid drap' herself and then gave a little to each of the babies. 'My goodness, child,' said my mother to the wee thing that was trotting at her mother's side. 'Doesn't it bite you?' 'Ay, but I like the bite,' replied the creature.'

Throughout Scotland, from the Highlands to the Borders, whisky was illicitly distilled in enormous quantities. The Statistical Account is full of mentions of it and there was virtually nothing anyone could do about it. Producing whisky was almost the only way the farmers could dispose of their surplus barley. The illicit distiller and the smugglers went about their business unhindered by anyone save the Gaugers against whom everyone's hand was turned. An Act of 1786 had imposed duty on whisky sent to England, which merely increased the smuggling. An Act of 1814 prohibited any stills under 500 gallons, which Major General David Stewart of Garth in his *Sketches of the Character, Manners and Present State of the Highlanders* written in 1822, pointed out: 'was a complete interdict, as a still of this magnitude would consume more than the disposable grain in the most extensive county . . .'

In 1823, a total of 1,400 illicit stills were discovered by the Excise officials, which gives a fair idea of the number operating that were not discovered. In the same year, however, an Act was passed which finally solved the problem. By granting the right to a forty gallon still for a licence fee of £10 and 2s 3d duty per gallon it at last had the effect of checking the number of illicit stills. By 1834 the number discovered was down to 692 and by 1874 to 6. A farmer named George Smith in Glenlivet was amongst the first persuaded to take out a licence in 1824. The future of good Scotch whisky was assured.

In 1845 Charles St. John the celebrated naturalist and sportsman of the 19th century described a night spent in a 'whiskie bothie' when with his servant Donald he found himself benighted while in pursuit of a giant stag known as 'The Muckle Hart of Benmore'. It was dark and pouring with rain in the middle of a wild moor when he was astounded to hear what sounded like a fiddle. He mentioned this to Donald who was delighted:

'It's all right enough, sir; just follow the sound; it's that drunken deevil, Sandy Ross; ye'll never haud a fiddle frae him, nor him frae a whisky-still'.

After wading waist deep across a burn in spate with their guns held high and clinging on to each other they finally scrambled up the other side:

'Following the merry sound we came to what seemed a mere hole in the bank, from which it proceeded. The hole was partially close by a door woven of heather . . . On a barrel in the middle of the apartment – half hut, half cavern – stood aloft, fiddling with all his might, the identical Sandy Ross, while round him danced three unkempt savages; and another figure was stooping, employed over a fire in the corner, where the whisky pot was in full operation. The fire, and a sliver or two of lighted bog fir, gave light enough to see the whole, for the place was not above ten feet square. We made our approaches with becoming caution, and were, needless to say, hospitably received; for who ever heard of Highland smugglers refusing a welcome to sportsmen? We got rest, food and fire – all we required – and something more; for long after I had betaken me to the dry heather in the corner, I had disturbed visions of strange orgies in the bothie, and of my sober Donald exhibiting curious antics on the top of a tub . . . when daylight awoke me, the smugglers and Donald were all quiet and asleep, far past my efforts to arouse them, with the exception of one who was still able to tend the fire under the large black pot. From the state in which my trusty companion was, with his head in a heap of ashes, I saw it would serve no purpose to wake him, even if I were able to do so. It was quite clear he would be good for nothing all day. I therefore . . . departed with my rifle alone . . .'

After another two days and a night spent in the open, St. John shot his 'Muckle Hart'. Such epic stalks were not the lot of many sportsmen, but his book *Wild Sports and Natural History of the Highlands* ran into nine editions and encouraged yet more people to visit the Highlands. In the latter half of the 19th century the fame of the Highland scenery, as well as the attractions of the fishing, shooting and stalking were bringing increasing numbers to the Highlands. Numerous wealthy English sportsmen were buying estates and building shooting lodges, following the example of 'the dear Queen'. Deer were replacing the sheep which had been the cause of the eviction of so many Highlanders whose crofts were now marked only by heaps of stones and the greenness of the land around them. The few Highlanders remaining were employed as ghillies, stalkers and in similar posts.

The sports which the Highlanders had delighted in, the trials of strength, wrestling, racing up the hills to a mark and down again, putting the stone, throwing the hammer, tossing the caber, pipe playing and Highland dancing were organised in annual games. The Highland Games as well as the Highland dress became a potent attraction to the annual visitors. The English had taken over the Highlands and were busy reorganising them in their own image.

Yet not all things Highland could be thus organised. The Manhood Stones, such as that at Inver, the Clad Cuid Fir, remained merely a remarkable spectacle of the past. Even more remarkable are the Dinnie Stones at the Bridge of Potarch. These weigh over 785 lbs. between them and the feat is to lift both and carry them across the bridge. Not surprisingly it is one seldom performed. It was said to be a MacCrimmon of Skye who lifted the largest Clad Cuid Fir ever known and placed his belt underneath it as a reward for anyone who could repeat the feat. Nearly a century later argument arose about the possibility of such an effort and the stone was raised with lifting devices to find the remains of the belt still in position.

By the late 19th century the Highland sporting Inn had begun to be recognisable as its modern counterpart. Catering primarily for sportsmen rather than travellers it would be sited near good fishing, stalking or shooting frequently far from the main road or any passing traveller's convenience. Inside, it was varnished a dark brown, which grew darker with each passing year, and furnished with leather armchairs suitable for tweed-clad sportsmen. On the walls preserved specimens of record trout and salmon began to appear with occasional heads of exceptional deer interspersed between them. Glass cases containing stuffed capercailzie, grouse, ptarmigan, wild cats and other fauna of the Highlands were another favourite form of decoration.

The large dish in the hall to accept offerings from sportsmen on the river or the loch, usually placed beneath the barometer which everyone consulted and tapped when leaving or entering, was an essential item of furniture. The deer larder outside to take the carcases from the hill was usually sited alongside the game larder, both suitably meshed against the perennial pests of the Highlands, the flies. Large airing cupboards and outhouses were required for wet clothes, hobnailed boots and similar sporting paraphernalia. The gun-room and rod-room and kennels for the dogs, boathouses, stables and the inevitable coachhouse, eventually to be converted into garages, all these began to be an inseparable part of the normal Highland sporting Inn. Discreetly placed somewhere behind all this was the primitive bar for the ghillies, stalkers and other Highland helpers to take their dram after the day's sport.

Every year, another volume of bound *Punches* joined the steadily increasing row as suitable reading material for the unemployed sportsman on the Sabbath, when, of course, no fishing, shooting or stalking was permissible. Gradually, over the years, the varnish became darker, the leather armchairs more worn, and fresh fish or heads were added to the walls. Regularly, the same sportsmen came at the same time each year. The Highland Inn was in the making and it is perhaps understandable why it differed so completely from any other type of inn in Britain, save for a few Celtic Welsh fishing equivalents.

Chapter Twelve

Drink versus Temperance to 1970

Problem of drunkenness – Puritans originators of Temperance – Effects of Drink on History – Time Lag Law – Wesley and Wilberforce – Influence of U.S.A. – First Temperance Societies – Teetotal Pledge – Absurd Theories – Replies – Bands of Hope – Prohibition – Lawson – Gladstone's Acts – Magee – Better Free than Sober – Model Inns – 1908 Act defeated – Sir Victor Horsley – 1914 War – Opening Hours Restricted – Liquor Control Board – Nationalisation – Carlisle Scheme – Prohibition U.S.A. – True Temperance Association – Effect of Boy Scouts – Motor-Cars – Mergers – Sports

An Englishman's a man of parts,
He never drinks by fits and starts:
But once or twice a week maybe,
He'll go upon an evening's spree.
And after such an evening's revel,
He'll think himself the very devil.

WILLIAM BERNARD: Miscellaneous Verse: 1947.

FROM THE DAYS of the Saxon Kings through to the 20th century, control of excessive drinking was the perennial problem besetting almost every successive government in England. Frequent efforts were made, as we have seen, to control the proliferation of alehouses and tippling houses, the distillation of cheap spirits, or the smuggling of contraband wines and brandy, but mostly to little avail. Drunkards might be punished under the Tudors by being made to parade publicly in the 'Drunkard's Cloak', a barrel with the bottom knocked out and holes for arms, or under the Stuarts by six hours in the stocks, but with little effect. The problem was that much of the water was unfit to drink and a taste for ale, or wine, was acquired from an early age. Competitive drinking, leading to excess, remained a problem.

It was in the Puritan way of life and thought that the Temperance movements really had their origins. It was not, of course, that they were against ale, or wine, indeed many of them were brewers. Cromwell's mother was a brewster, hence his nickname 'Brewer'. He reduced the tax on whisky in Scotland and, albeit unwittingly, laid the foundations of the flourishing port trade of the 18th and 19th centuries. Even such biased commentators as Stubbs, who condemned the Maypoles and also condemned Church Ales as scenes 'where dronken Bacchus beares swaie' probably had a point on that score. It was not ale, or wine, they condemned but the abuse of it by excessive drinking, particularly competitive drinking, which led to so much drunkenness. By preaching that moderation was a virtue and drunkenness a sin they laid the foundations of the Temperance movements of the 19th century.

Prior to the Puritan regime of the Commonweath, ale and wine were the only alternatives to water. As a result many people probably passed their entire lives without drinking water in any significant quantities and also without ever being entirely sober. There are some grounds for thinking that it was only after the introduction of tea and coffee that sobriety became a recognisably permanent condition of life. It was not perhaps so much that people wished to get intoxicated, but that they found it difficult to remain quite sober. In such a condition it was easy to become involved unwittingly in a drinking session, as Pepys' diaries often indicated.

Although often overlooked, there can be little doubt that this is a factor which at times has very considerably influenced the history of these islands, and indeed the world. A good example was in 1203 when King John virtually surrendered Normandy and the Angevin lands in France to the French King Philip II by his failure to organise any defence at a crucial point in the campaign. The reason, according to the chroniclers, was that he was engaged in a prolonged drunken debauch. By 1204 Normandy was lost to England forever.

There are many other examples throughout our history up to the present day, which spring to mind as occasions when the sobriety of one or another of the principals might be questioned, or even that of the rank and file. Indeed, taking this into account, a great deal of what is often otherwise inexplicable begins to make sense. The Temperance pamphleteers of the 19th century fastened onto this idea with alacrity and rewrote the history of Britain beginning with the drunken ancient Britons being defected by 'very temperate' Romans and continuing in this vein. Like most humourless fanatics they carried it too far and conveniently ignored the converse that many daring acts of leadership in battle and some of the greatest feats of oratory in peace were directly inspired by alcohol. To have admitted this would have been to destroy the narrow core of Puritan prejudice on which their views were based.

Following the Puritan regime of the Commonwealth, the Restoration saw a swing back to heavy drinking again and then the introduction of spirit drinking on a scale never previously experienced. The really interesting feature of the Temperance Movements is that they did not start during the cheap gin era from 1720 to 1750 when many people were undoubtedly shocked and outraged at the evil and injurious effects of alcohol. Basically, however, the feeling of the times was against any interference with personal freedom, including the freedom to get drunk. Throughout the reigns of the three Georges and the Regency period heavy drinking remained the rule rather than the exception.

Once again what might be termed the 'Time Lag Law', which appeared to operate in all matters concerning the introduction of new drinks, or legislation concerning drink, seems to have taken effect. Although the Puritans preached moderation in the mid-17th century and the public conscience was undoubtedly outraged during the cheap gin era in the mid-18th century, it was not until well into the 19th century that the Temperance Movements began to emerge as coherent bodies.

Though Wesley and the evangelical movement of the 1780s were against excess spirit drinking, like their Puritan predecessors they were not against drinking ale and beer. Yet without the example of the methods used by evangelical humanitarians such as Wilberforce in swaying public opinion against the Slave Trade the Temperance Movements could hardly have started so spontaneously. Many of the same names were involved at the start and they were also joined initially by mill-owners and other industrialists, who saw in the Temperance Movements a more settled labour force and hence contributed their presence and business acumen.

Strangely enough, the first spur seems to have come from the United States, where around 1770 the Quakers began to agitate against drinking.

By the first decade of the 19th century pledges to abstain from drink were being sworn, although total abstention does not seem to have been introduced until around 1827. By 1829, however, American ships' captains were distributing temperance tracts in Liverpool. In the same year various Temperance Societies were formed in Greenock and Glasgow, both significantly also areas with strong American connections. By 1830 a Liverpool Temperance Society had been formed and the resoundingly titled British and Foreign Temperance Society based in London which was presided over by Charles Blomfield, the Bishop of London.

The time, the mood of the country and the people, were all ready for the rapid spread of Temperance Movements. To add impetus, if it had been required, the Duke of Wellington's Beer Act of 1830 resulted in an immediate and vast increase in the number of beer shops throughout the country and a consequent visible increase in drunkenness. The crusading, evangelical fervour of the temperance enthusiasts matched a need in the growing industrial towns, where there was little in the way of interest and light relief. The temperance tracts and temperance meetings provided a change, if nothing else, and soon the Temperance Movements were deluging the country with tracts and pamphlets. William Collins, a founder member of the Glasgow Temperance Society, and John Cassell in London were two publishers who were to make their fortunes from the printing and publication of temperance literature in the 19th century.

Until 1832 the temperance pledges had merely been for moderation in drinking. In 1832 the Preston Temperance Society, appropriately formed in the Old Cockpit in Preston, advocated total abstinence. In 1833 the term 'teetotal' was coined by a reformed drunkard named Turner and the real Temperance Movement was at last under way. The 'Lancashire fanatics' as they were termed were not at first popular in the south, but in the north they were immensely successful. In 1835 the Independent Order of Rechabites was formed as a friendly society with the usual sickness benefits and regular meetings, with the distinction that only teetotallers could belong. By 1834 they had a membership of 25,000. By 1850 the British and Foreign Temperance Society advocating merely moderation was wound up due to lack of support. The teetotallers had the field to themselves.

The suddenness and violence of the teetotallers' fervour had taken the brewers and the publicans by surprise. True, individual meetings were heckled, sometimes the speakers were mobbed, missiles were hurled and violent scenes took place, but the teetotallers continued to make converts successfully. It was not until the 1840s that any sort of effective opposition began to exploit the many absurd statements and claims put forward by ill-educated teetotallers, such as the theory that as:

'Four pints of beer would make a man drunk, two pints would make him half drunk . . . half a pint would make him half a quarter drunk, consequently they were all drunkards.'

In 1846 the teetotallers own effective tactics were copied and a tract entitled *A Medical, Moral and Christian dissection of teetotallers* was published, with illustrations by the cartoonist Phiz. This was the first broadside from the drinking lobby. Then in 1849 a lapsed teetotaller, Thomas Smeeton, published his *Confessions of a Convert from Teetotalism to Temperance,* in which he wrote:

'The Rechabite Societies are nearly all broken up through the wranglings and intemperate squabbles of the brethren. The meetings of many temperance committees, as I painfully know, are little more than arenas for the display of hatred and all uncharitableness.'

Still Temperance was steadily gaining ground and fresh converts to its cause. The most important step in the entire movement was the formation in 1847 of the first Band of Hope, or junior branch, pledged not to take alcohol. At a time when there was absolutely no form of organised entertainment for the young this was an immediate success. By 1876 there were 5,500 Bands of Hope with 800,000 members. By 1900 there were 16,000 with over two million members. Although unquestionably many lapsed on becoming adults these numbers are sufficient to explain the power of the Temperance Movement at the turn of the century. Constant awards for the best Essay on Temperance and the dissemination of vast amounts of propaganda from edifying stories for the young to revised histories of Britain helped to instil the Temperance message in the schools. In all the late Victorian and Edwardian schoolboy stories it was invariably the badge of the 'rotter' that he was seen 'entering a public house'. It was amongst the young that the Temperance Movement won its greatest victories.

The advent of Prohibition in Maine in 1851 resulted in even more intensive efforts by many British teetotallers to spread their message. Lecture tours by eloquent evangelists, regular meetings and ever more tracts and pamphlets were the principal means employed. The ultimate aims, however, of many in the Temperance Movement now began to diverge. Some wanted total Prohibition. Others maintained that they would be content with the prohibition of the sale of drink, allowing people to brew their own beer if they wished. Yet others were content with moderate drinking. Vicious internal conflicts and dissensions became a marked feature of certain sections of the movement. Soon these were to become public to the detriment of their cause.

Amongst the many cranks, fanatics and honest converts attracted to the Temperance Movement one of the most unlikely in many ways was Wilfrid Lawson, M.P. Son of a wealthy, progressive and teetotal baronet, who on his conversion to teetotalism had poured all his gin into his fish-ponds, Wilfrid Lawson was himself teetotal. He was also an enthusiastic, witty and sporting Master of Foxhounds in Northumberland where his father's estates covered a considerable acreage. Sir Wilfrid Lawson, as he became on his father's death in 1867, appreciated the danger of the Temperance Movement splitting up and maintained that if this did not happen they would 'be in at the death of the liquor traffic'. He went on to pillory recently created peers as 'men who had killed a lot of people in battle . . . or . . . brewed a lot of beer', castigating the brewers wittily as 'the beerage'. Popular in spite of his views he became the acknowledged leader of the Temperance Movement.

In 1860 Gladstone reduced the duty on French wines, both in an attempt to increase trade with France and because he was convinced that the solution to drunkenness lay in encouraging wine drinking. In 1861, being a confirmed believer in Free Trade he also virtually threw the off-licence wine trade open to anyone. In this course he was opposed not only by the Temperance Movement, but also by the Brewers and Publicans, who for once found themselves unexpected allies in this matter with the Temperance supporters. In the end he merely managed to found the fortunes of the firm of Messrs. Gilbey and Sons, who promptly set up a chain of local suppliers throughout the country. Although wine drinking increased the figures showed that in fact all drinking also increased, thus on all counts his efforts were highly unsuccessful.

In 1864 Wilfrid Lawson moved a Bill to allow the owners of land and property in certain areas to have the right to prevent the sale of drink by a two-thirds majority. This 'local option' principle met with instant opposition from both sides of Parliament and was resoundingly voted out. It also had the effect of making Lawson thoroughly unpopular throughout the country and in the following year he lost his seat. He was not, however, a man easily deterred and he tub-thumped throughout the country for the following three years until returned again in 1868. He then resolutely introduced the same Bill again and once more it was resoundingly defeated.

In the same year, 1869, the Wine and Beer House Act was introduced, which had the effect of limiting the increasing number of beer shops. It thus, incidentally, increased the value of those already in existence and resulted in an undignified scramble by the brewers to tie up the remainder as they realised the importance of securing the remaining retail outlets for their beer. This Private Members Bill was perhaps Gladstone's most effective piece of licensing legislation, although not necessarily achieving the results intended.

In 1872 the government at last produced an enormous projected Bill entitled The Intoxicating Liquors Bill, which contained proposals for raising the licence duty, restricting the number of licences and opening hours, also suppressing any licences over a given number within a ten-year period without compensation. Surprisingly the Temperance Movement decried it as insufficiently far-reaching and failed to give it their support. Not surprisingly the brewers and licensed trade raised a storm of protest.

Easily the Bill's most outstanding critic was the Bishop of Peterborough, Dr. William Magee, subsequently Archbishop of York, who decried it on the grounds that if offered the choice of England free or sober, he would think it: 'better that England should be free, than that England should be compulsorily sober'. The catch-phrase 'Better Free than Sober' was soon displayed on the walls of public houses and shouted at every temperance meeting. By the time the Temperance Movement had changed its mind and decided to support the Bill it was already too late. The Bill had been withdrawn. When Gladstone was subsequently defeated in the 1874 election by Disraeli he wrote to his brother: 'we have been borne down in a torrent of gin and beer'.

Repeated attempts by Sir Wilfrid Lawson and others to introduce similar bills were failures for one reason or another and government after government shirked the issue. The principal difficulty was that so many changing factors seemed to be the key to the problem. The entire question of licensing was an involved one. If the number of licences was to be reduced then the subject of compensation payable and the amounts to be paid in turn appeared to pose insuperable problems. Among the many different stumbling blocks presented, the real questions as to whether drunkenness in reality caused poverty, or whether more licences resulted in more drunkenness, the answer to both of which was negative, were completely ignored, or overlooked.

Perhaps the major stumbling block, which so many dedicated teetotallers never overcame, was their own narrowness of outlook and imagination. When the Rev. Osbert Mordaunt in 1876 attempted to run a model public house and succeeded on a small scale in doing so, he was decried for making drinking respectable. Their ideal, too often, was the absurd one of a public house with the maximum discomfort for the drinker who patronised it. They openly stated that the provision of games and other entertainments was to be discouraged in conjunction with the sale of drinks. They approved the Swedish experiment at Gothenburg which attempted to discourage drinking by short hours, high prices, gloomy establishments and drinking mugs shaped like medicine glasses. Such humourless and negative attitudes were bound in the end to be self-defeating. For all that, their agitation for reforms, ranging from prohibition downwards, continued unabated.

In 1904 the Conservative government of the day introduced a Bill for compensation to be paid for licences suppressed over a period of years, which was duly passed. In 1908 the Liberal government which succeeded them with Asquith as Chancellor of the Exchequer proposed a much more drastic and far-reaching Bill, which envisaged suppression of a full third of the 100,000 licences in England and Wales and the immediate introduction of 'local option', by which an area could vote itself 'dry'. Compensation was to be raised from the trade itself and shared out by a Licensing Commission. The immediate effect throughout the country was mixed. The Temperance Movements greeted it with pleasure and the rest of the country with outrage. At by-elections the government lost every seat by enormous margins. In the event the House of Lords, exercising their option, rejected the Bill with a resounding majority.

The year 1908 also saw the publication of a quite remarkable pseudo-medical and scientific publication entitled *Alcohol and the Human Body*, by Sir Victor Horsley in conjunction with Dr. Mary Sturge, both self-confessed opponents of drinking. The title page proclaimed boldly: 'Alcohol is a poison – so is strychnine, so is arsenic'. The first chapter was entitled 'Alcohol is a Drug'. The authors detailed experiments they had conducted on plants and animals. Alcohol they found killed plants treated with it and also jellyfish. They solemnly detailed the effects of drink on dogs as recorded by two American professors, which proved conclusively to their satisfaction that drunken dogs were less efficient at retrieving balls than sober dogs.

This remarkable publication soon attracted some scathing comment, in particular that of Dr. C. A. Mercier, who wrote:

'To do the authors justice they make no pretence of impartiality. They set out with the intention of showing that alcohol in any form or in any quantity is wholly, unmitigatedly and irredeemably vile. I find from their book that vegetables when they are watered with alcohol . . . wither and die; and I resolved at once that never in future will I water my cabbages with Chateau Mouton Rothschild . . . If we are to abjure alcohol because it is injurious to cabbages, it would be a good plan to drink diluted sewage, which is so beneficial to them.'

No doubt such exchanges between Temperance supporters and their opponents could have continued indefinitely, but for the outbreak of war in 1914. It was this which finally led to the greatest changes in the country's drinking habits since the days of the Saxons. The Intoxicating Liquor (Temporary Restrictions) Bill was passed in 1914 almost at once, although not without suggestions that the government was attempting to make up for its defeat over its Bill of 1908 and assurances from the Home Secretary that Prohibition would not be put forward except as an emergency measure. The immediate effects of this Bill were dramatic. The shorter opening hours it introduced, from 8 a.m. to 10 p.m., or 11 p.m. in London, instead of 5 a.m. to 12.30 a.m. had remarkable results in reducing drunkenness at closing time, which previously had been considerable. Even the Brewer's Gazette admitted that it was 'A transformation'.

The tax on beer was raised and the strength of beer was reduced. The price of spirits, similarly diluted, was also raised even more drastically. It became an offence to treat anyone to a drink in a bar and people were sent to prison for breaking the law in this respect. Even the rum ration to the British Army came under attack. However the most serious problem, and a genuine one, was the high incidence of drunkenness amongst workers making munitions or in the shipyards. Lloyd George in 1915 claimed: 'Drink is doing more damage in the War than all the German submarines put together'. He said also: 'We are fighting Germany, Austria and drink and the greatest of these deadly foes is drink.'

He contemplated nationalising the breweries and public houses at a cost of £250 millions, but eventually under the Defence of the Realm Act decided to appoint a Central Liquor Control Board which was to have powers to close the public houses in a designated area, and if required build and run its own breweries and public houses, controlling opening hours and sale of spirits. It was also empowered to pay compensation, but without any appeal against its decisions. The Bill for this far-reaching act was passed almost without dissension. Predictably, perhaps, the only voices raised against it were those of the Prohibitionists, who claimed that the government had no right to experiment in such a way.

In 1916 the Board nationalised an area of fifty square miles around

Carlisle and set up a state management scheme controlling the inns and producing beer from their own brewery. The number of public houses was drastically reduced and the laws strictly enforced, including that of 'No Treating'. Some idea of the effects of the scheme can be gained from the fact that the leading prohibitionist, Leif Jones, M.P., admitted rather grudgingly that the Board had made the bar 'as uncomfortable and unattractive as they can'.

Although by 1916 the pre-war consumption of beer had been cut from thirty-six million barrels a year to twenty-six millions, the government were wisely advised against reducing it by a further ten millions in 1917. A Commission of Inquiry set up to investigate the matter found that lack of beer was a major source of industrial discontent so the decision was made instead to brew another six million gallons. Even so by 1918 the consumption of drink in all its varied forms had fallen from a pre-war 1914 figure of 89 million gallons to a mere 37 million gallons. The result of shorter opening hours, higher prices of drink, and sheer shortage, had effected more than all the Temperance Movements or the governments of the previous centuries.

By 1918 despite the deliberate policy of the Board to make their public houses uncomfortable for drinkers, a policy long advocated by Temperance supporters, the Carlisle experiment was proving a success. The overall profit of the scheme was fifteen per cent, a figure considerably better than most commercial concerns. Inevitably the scheme was continued under the control of the Home Office and in particular the emergent Labour Party was confirmed in its belief that the nationalisation of the trade was the ultimate solution. The fact that there was a soulless, antiseptic atmosphere about such State-owned concerns was by the way. With a system of tied houses they had in effect 'tied' drinkers, who, if they wanted a drink at all, had to put up with the local conditions. The same danger, of course, is apparent with too large a monopoly by any commercial brewer.

With the introduction of Prohibition in the U.S.A. in 1920, a move was at once made to try to enforce prohibition in this country. Various speakers were brought over from the U.S.A., but little success was achieved beyond the surprising defeat of Winston Churchill by a 'prohibition candidate' Mr. E. Scrymgeour at Dundee in 1922. He tried to introduce a Prohibition Bill in Parliament but it was roundly rejected by 236 votes to 14.

Although the threat of prohibition was never really likely to materialise it was enough to cause the brewers and publicans to unite formidably for the first time in order to fight back. Once again the 'Time Lag Law' operated. Now that the threat was virtually in the past the drink trade began to exert itself and unite in its own defence. The True Temperance Association was formed and *True Temperance Monographs* was published in 1921, which effectively demolished most cherished Temperance theories, such as the fact that habitual criminals were heavy drinkers, it being observed that in fact most criminals in the slums drank cocoa. For the first time the real reasons for drinking were soundly advocated by a mental specialist, who wrote:

'What the great majority of people drink alcohol for is not because they like the taste of it, nor because they are thirsty, but . . . because it makes them feel jolly.'

In 1932 a *Handbook for Speakers and Writers on the So-called Temperance Question* was produced. This proved that drink was not responsible for poverty, that it did not cause crime, or ill-treatment of children. It also proved that teetotalism was in its way a menace. It pointed to the effects of Prohibition in driving the young onto drugs in the U.S.A. These and many other points were effectively made, but the time for such a document was already nearly over. The Temperance Movement had nearly shot its bolt. The failure of Prohibition and its repeal in 1933 was the final straw.

There were several outside factors at work undermining the strength of the Temperance Movements, apart from the fact that they were now fighting a battle which had been already won, with almost all their aims achieved and drunkenness no longer a problem of any magnitude. The Bands of Hope meanwhile had been steadily losing ground. The more attractive and interesting activities of the Boy Scout Movement under the leadership of Baden Powell had proved an insidious lure to their prospective membership. By the late 1930s they were virtually non-existent and with them had vanished a great percentage of the possible members of the Temperance Movements of the future.

In the 1930s the effects of the motor-car first began to be perceived. The new type of road-house inn was introduced, aimed principally at the motorist. Chromium plating, showy furnishings and plush carpeting replaced old, but not unattractive coaching inns. The brewers vied with each other in producing such new attractions as they conceived them. Fortunately some retained a sense of proportion and not all old inns were necessarily condemned or renovated beyond recognition. Despite this trend a great deal remained to be done as late as the 1940s in the way of improving sanitation in many public houses throughout the country, even to the extent, in some cases, of laying on a piped water supply.

Temperance propaganda, in reverse

The Landlord of the "Grapes" emptying the casks and demolishing the bottles in his cellar.

The effects of the Second World War, beyond inevitable shortages, were nothing like as severe as those of the First World War. Apart from a series of distribution schemes reorganising brewery delivery areas, which chiefly affected the trade, and apart from the loss of a number of public houses by bombing, there was little noticeable effect on the public or on their drinking habits. The sporting life of the inn, or public house, continued much as before, only less drink of weaker strength and higher price was consumed.

In 1948 the Socialist post-war government passed a Bill introducing State Management in all public houses in new towns. They did not, however, nationalise the entire trade. Nor was the measure long in being, for the de-humanising influence of such a scheme was soon apparent to all. In 1952 the new town public houses were de-nationalised by the ensuing Conservative government.

Throughout the 1950s and 1960s the breweries indulged in further massive amalgamations and mergers. The process, which had begun in the late 18th century, appeared, after the inevitable operation of the 'Time Lag Law', to be reaching its conclusion. Short of integration into even larger combines, or near monopolies, the process appeared to have reached its ultimate end by the late 1960s. Plastic hoses and metal pressure beer containers replaced old wooden barrels. Lighter bottled beers, identical except for their labels, replaced old known favourites as local breweries were swallowed up and ceased to exist. In tied areas the local drinker had little or no choice.

The enormous traffic on the roads during the same period brought trade and life to many inns and public houses which previously had been moribund. Fake beams, horse brasses and coach horns proliferated as in the 1930s. Although the introduction of the breathalyser in 1967, as a curb on drunken driving, was a questionable cure for road accidents, it combined with the spread of television during the 1960s to force the breweries and the publicans to introduce further attractions to their establishments to continue to draw custom. More pin-tables, soft drinks, soft music and greater comfort were all indirect and mainly successful attempts to woo the customer from his own T.V. set at home.

In 1971 the Carlisle scheme was finally wound up. Although it had proved that such a venture can be run successfully it had also shown that when the State takes over what is essentially a personal relationship between one man and another, as between landlord and customer, something is lost. Whether inn, tavern, alehouse, tippling house or public house, the relationship between landlord and customer has remained much the same over the ages. With the introduction of a paid manager much of this relationship is lost, for they cannot have the same feeling of personal involvement. To the credit of the brewers the majority of them appreciate this point, although it is not always possible to obtain independent landlords for their tied houses.

Understandably any demand for a return to longer opening hours is opposed by the publicans, who have little enough time to themselves as it is. They also appreciate that the price of drink would inevitably rise to balance the increased cost of service during the extra hours with perhaps little gain to them. Whatever may result on that score the general public will suffer most should there be any further giant mergers between combines with vast interests outside the drink trade, for this would be on a par with nationalisation and would ultimately spell the end of the inn and the public house as we know them today.

Surprisingly, despite all the changes that have taken place, the sports of the inns have not changed unduly. Even ring-the-bull and the-devil-among-the-tailors are still practised in isolated country inns. Such varied activities as knur and spell, stoolball or bat and trap are also still played at one or two inns. Darts, dominoes and various forms of card games are still favourite standbyes. In some places one-armed bandits, the mechanised form of dice, are to be found and various types of pin-ball are common, both dating back in origin for centuries. There are also still public houses in London with their own theatres attached, or with their shows of various kinds, produced as a counter attraction to television. There is even an inn in north Norfolk the landlord of which is national champion funny face puller. All else may change but tastes remain the same. People still go to inns and public houses to drink and disport themselves with gaiety, games, gossip and song. Long may it continue so.

Fuinness

Bibliography

Pre 1900

Anonymous. *A Friendly Admonition to Drinkers of Brandy, etc.*, 1733
Bickerdyke, J. *The Curiosities of Ale & Beer*, 1886
Boorde, Andrew. *A Dyetary of Health*, 1542
Burns, James Dawson. *History of Temperance, Two vols.*, 1881–1890
Burt, Captain Edward. *Letters from a Gentleman in the North of Scotland to his Friend in London*, 1724–1728
Burton, Robert. *The Anatomy of Melancholy*, 1621
Byng, Hon. John. *The Torrington Diaries*, 1781–1794
Chaucer. *Canterbury Tales*, 1388
Cobbett, William. *Rural Rides*, 1821
Cotton, Charles. *The Compleat Gamester*, 1674
Cowling, Samuel. *History of the Temperance Movement*, 1862
Daniel, The Rev. William Barker. *Rural Sports*, 1801
Defoe, Daniel. *A Tour through England & Wales*, 1724–1728
De la Rochefoucauld, François. *A Frenchman in England; or Mélanges sur l'Angleterre*, 1784
Esquiros, H. F. *Journey in England*, 1861
Evelyn, John. *Memoirs*
Flecknoe, Richard. *Heroic Portraits with other Miscellany Pieces*, 1660
French, Richard V. *Nineteen Centuries of Drink in England*, 1862
Gomme, Alice. *The Traditional Games of England, Ireland and Scotland*, 1894
Grant, Elizabeth of Rochiemurchus. *Memoirs of a Highland Lady*, 1797–1827
Harrison. *Description of England*, 1583
Hawker, Col. Thomas. *Diaries*, 1782–1851
Heywood. *Philocothonista, or the Drunkard Opened, dissected and anatomised*, 1635
Kitchiner, W. *Traveller's Oracle*, 1826
Langland, William. *Piers Plowman*, *c.* 1362
Maitland, W. *History of London*, 1739
Mathias, P. *The Brewing Industry in England 1730–1830*, 1897
Morison, Fynes. *Itinerary*, 1605–1617
Moritz, Pastor Carl Philipp. *Travels in England*, 1782

Morwyng, Peter. *Treasure of Evynomous*, 1559
Osbaldestone. *Reminiscences*
Pennant, Thomas. *Pennant's Tours*, 1776
Pepys, Samuel. *Diaries*, 1660–1689
Pole, W. *Handbook of Games*, 1890
Richardson, J. *The Philosophical Principles of Brewing*, 1784
Russom, J. *Evil Effects of Beer shops*, 1849
St. John, Charles. *Wild Sports & Natural History of the Highlands*, 1845
Samuelson, J. *The History of Drink*, 1878
Shadwell, Arthur. *Drink, Temperance and Legislation*, 1903
Shaw, Dr. *The Juice of the Grape; Or Wine Preferable to Water*, 1724
Sinclair, Sir Archibald, Bt. *Statistical Account of Scotland*, 1791–1799
Stewart, Major General David of Garth. *Sketches of the Character, Manners & Present State of the Highlanders*, 1822
Strutt, Joseph. *Sports & Pastimes of the People of England*, 1801
Taylor, E. *History of Playing Cards*, 1765
Taylor, John. *Pennyless Pilgrimage*, 1649
Thornton, Thomas. *Highland Tour*, 1784 (published 1805)
Tryon, Thomas. *The Way to Health, Long Life & Happiness*, 1691
Vaughan, William. *Directions for Health*, 1600
Wickham Legg, A. G. (Editor). *A Survey of Twenty-Six Counties in Seven Weeks by a Captain, a Lieutenant and an Ensign*, 1904

Post 1900

Askwith, Lord. *British Taverns: Their History and Laws*, 1928
Bartlett, Vernon. *The Past of Pastimes*, 1969
Batchelor, Denzil. *The English Inn*, 1963
Bradford, Sarah. *The Englishman's Wine*, 1969
Burke, Thomas. *Travel in England*, 1942
Day, Wentworth J. *Watney Book of Inns of Sport*, 1949
Delderfield, R. L. *British Inn Signs*, 1965
Eberlein and Richardson. *The English Inn, Past & Present*, 1925
Finn, T. *Watney Book of Pub Games*, 1967
Harrison, Brian. *Drink and the Victorians*, 1971
Henderson, *History of Ancient and Modern Wines*, 1944
Hindley. *Tavern Anecdotes*
Hoyle, Edmund. *Encyclopedia of Games*, 1950
Keverne, Richard, with Hammond Innes. *Tales of Old Inns*, 1939
Longmate, Norman. *The Waterdrinkers*, 1968

Monkton, H. A. *A History of English Ale and Beer*, 1966
Monkton, H. A. *A History of the English Public House*, 1968
Parkes, J. *Travel in England in the 17th century*
Richardson, A. E. *The Old Inns of England*, 1934
Salzman, L. F. *English Life in the Middle Ages*, 1926
Simon, Andre. *Drink*, 1948
Trevelyan, G. M. *English Social History*, 1944
True Temperance Monographs. True Temperance Association, 1921
Wymer, Norman. *Sport in England*, 1949

Research

In the course of his life-long research for this book, the author has had happy occasion to note in particular the following hostelries:

ABERDEENSHIRE

Braemar: *Mar Lodge*; converted Gothic baronial shooting lodge once belonging to the Duke of Fife.

ANGLESEY

Beaumaris: *Ye Olde Bull's Head*; posting inn dated 1472, with a yard. Roundhead's HQ associated with Dickens and Dr. Johnson.

ARGYLLSHIRE

Ardbrecknish: *Ardbrecknish House*; trout fishing in Loch Awe. Salmon and sea trout fishing; roughshooting and deer-stalking.

Clachan Seil: *Tigh-an-Truish*; called the 'House of the Trouser' because the Highlanders on leave from the army used to change from their trousers into their kilts here before going home.

Glencoe: *King's House*; Scotland's oldest licensed inn. Used as a barracks by the Redcoats after Culloden. Fishing, shooting, stalking. Bowling alley.

Strachur: *Creggans Inn*; 400 years old. Fishing on Loch Fyne. Riding.

Taynuilt: *Inverinan Lodge*; trout fishing, ghillie available. Stalking, roughshooting and riding.

BANFFSHIRE

Craigellachie: *Craigellachie Inn*; 3 miles of fishing on the Spey.

Tomintoul: *Richmond Arms*; salmon and sea trout fishing on the Avon. Shooting.

BEDFORDSHIRE

Bedford: *Lion*; old posting house used as a recruiting centre in the 17th century.

Bletsoe: *Falcon*; once courthouse, farmhouse and posting house. Fishing on the Ouse.

Eaton Socon: *White Horse*; Georgian coaching inn frequented by fishermen, fox-hunters and shooting men.

Luton: *Red Lion*; ancient inn, once a monastery, then a posting house.

Woburn: *Bedford Arms*; Georgian inn rebuilt 1724. Big stables.

BERKSHIRE

Abingdon: *Crown and Thistle*; 18th century with fishing on the Thames.

Binfield: *Stag and Hounds*; 14th-century coaching inn, once a hunting lodge.

Binfield Heath: *Bottle and Glass*; 15th century, once a meeting place for Roundheads.

Boulter's Lock: *Boulter's Inn*; on an island in the Thames. Fishing.

Cholsey: *Brentford Tailor*; once used by travelling tailors.

Hurley: *Bell*; one of the oldest inns in England. Galleried.

Long Wittenham: *Barley Mow*; very old thatched inn on the Thames.

Stanford Dingley: *Bull*; 15th-century inn where ring the bull is still played.

Tidmarsh: *Greyhound*; *c.* 1220. The Garth and S. Berks. Hunt meet here.

Waltham St. Lawrence: *Bell*; 500 years old with overhanging eaves.

Windsor: *Castle*: posting house visited by the Duke of Wellington in 1814.

Winkfield: *White Hart*; 16th century. A stream runs through the huge cellar.

Wokingham: *Three Frogs*; 17th century.

BERWICKSHIRE

Duns: *White Swan*; old inn with hunting traditions.

Lauder: *Black Bull*; old coaching house catering for the sportsman.

BRECKNOCK

Brecon: *Shoulder of Mutton*: the birthplace of Sarah Siddons.

Llyswen: *Griffin*; village inn dated 1429. Salmon fishing on the Wye.

BUCKINGHAMSHIRE

Amersham: *Crown*; timbered coaching inn with a yard.

Beaconsfield: *Royal Standard of England*; part 13th century. HQ for the Royalists in the Civil War.

Colnbrook: *Ostrich*; Elizabethan building on a very old site.

Ford: *Dinton Hermit*; old inn connected with a famous recluse.

Great Missenden: *Nag's Head*; once a waggoners' halt.

Hartwell: *Bugle Horn;* ancient building, previously a winestore, then a farmhouse.

Medmenham: *Ye Old Dog and Badger*; 14th century. Once a badger hunting centre.

Red Pits: *Hare and Hounds*; old coaching inn where quoits was played.

West Wycombe: *George and Dragon*; 14th-century inn, said to be haunted. Secret passages and a priest's hole. Cromwell once stayed here.

Wheeler End: *Brickmakers Arms*; an old well under the lounge.

CAERNARVON

Capel Curig: *Tyn-y-Coed*; salmon and trout fishing. Shooting.

Conway: *Castle*; coaching inn with a cockpit and stables.

CAITHNESS

Loch Dubh: *Lochdhu*; trout and salmon fishing, falconry, grouse shooting and stalking.

CAMBRIDGESHIRE

Bartlow: *Three Hills*; old inn near three Saxon burial mounds.

Cambridge: *Blue Boar*; old coaching and posting inn with 15th-century cellars.
Eagle; large galleried yard.

Grantchester: *Red Lion*; Georgian inn known by Rupert Brooke.

CARDIGAN

Devil's Bridge: *Hafod Arms*; fishing through the Aberystwyth Angling Club.

CHESHIRE

Broxton: *Travel Inn*; 16th century.

Bucklow Hill: *Swan*; once famed for trotting horses.

Chester: *Bear and Billet*; half timbered inn built in 1664.
Falcon; old timbered inn with an overhanging upper storey.

Knutsford: *Royal George*; 14th century.

Peover: *Bells of Peover*; 13th-century church building, once frequented by highwaymen.

CORNWALL

Bodmin: *Hole-in-the-Wall*; once the Debtor's Prison.

Bolventor: *Jamaica Inn*; very old coaching inn on Bodmin Moor.

Bude: *Carriers Inn*; oldest house in Bude. Once frequented by wreckers.

Callington: *Bull's Head*; over 500 years old. Connected by a passage, once used by smugglers, to the church.

Crafthole: *Finneygook*; 400 years old. Supposed to be haunted by a smuggler.

Crantock: *Old Albion*; 16th-century thatched smugglers' inn built over a deep rock well.

Dartmoor: *Warren*; very isolated house, once used by tin mine workers.

Helston: *Angel*; a stone from Hell is in the wall, hence the name of the town.

Marazion: *Fire Engine*; a tunnel runs to a house across the street.

Mithian: *Miners Arms*; over four centuries old, with a tunnel and a secret room. Once a monks' retreat house.

Morwenstowe: *Bush*; 13th-century wreckers' and smugglers' inn. Celtic carvings on the wall.

Mousehole: *Lobster Pot*; sea and shark fishing.

Padstow: *London Inn*; originally a cottage alehouse.

Penzance: *Dolphin*; 600 years old; free trading inn with a secret room and a hiding place. Judge Jeffreys held court here.

Perran-Ar-Worthal: *Norway Inn*; old alehouse near Truro.

CORNWALL continued

Phillack: *New Inn*; 12th-century building with a 5th-century carving.

Pillaton: *Weary Friar*; 12th-century rest place for travelling friars.

Portscatho: *Plume of Feathers*; 17th-century fishing inn with a smugglers' hiding place in the chimney.

Restronguet Creek: *Pandora*; 13th-century fishing inn.

Saint Columb: *Ring o' Bells*; 13th century. Hurling matches played here.

Stratton: *Tree Inn*; Famed for a 7 foot 4 inch giant born here in 1610.

Trebarwith: *Mill House Inn*; once a flour mill. The mill wheel is still in position.

Trevaunance Cove: *Driftwood Spars*; parts from old wrecks.

Truro: *Heron*; converted cottages. Fishing.

CUMBERLAND

Bassenthwaite: *Pheasant*; fishing and shooting.

Boot: *Burnmoor*; fishing. Devoke Water (famous for its trout) is nearby.

Great Salkeld: *Highland Drove*; ancient inn with longstanding hunting tradition.

Keswick: *George*; oldest inn in the town. Once an ore smuggling centre.

Penrith: *Gloucester Arms*; Richard the Third often slept here.

Wastwater; *Wastwater Inn*; once a halfway house for ore and liquor smugglers.

DENBIGHSHIRE

Denbigh: *Bull*; Elizabethan timbered inn known by Dr. Johnson.

Ruthin: *Castle*; part 17th-century, part 18th-century coaching and posting inn.

DERBYSHIRE

Bakewell: *Rutland Arms*; on the Wye. Known by Jane Austen.

Ilam (nr. Ashbourne): *Izaak Walton*; farmhouse inn with trout and grayling fishing.

Matlock: *New Bath*; 18th-century house built round a hot lime spring.

Nr. Sheffield: *Scotsman's Pack*; used by travelling packmen and Scotsmen selling tweeds.

DEVONSHIRE

Bantham: *Sloop*; 16th-century inn. Trout and salmon fishing on the Avon.

Barnstaple: *Three Tuns*; old house with a Great Hall.

Berrynarbor; *Ye Olde Globe*; converted from three old beamed cottages.

Bickleigh: *Fisherman's Cot*; thatched inn on the Exe. Exclusive salmon and trout fishing.

Bideford: *Royal*; partly converted from a workhouse and a prison. 17th century oak staircase.

Branscombe: *Ye Olde Mason's Arms*; very old inn converted from cottages, with thatched porches.

Christow: *Artichoke*; 13th century. Once used by the Crusaders.

Combe-in-Teignhead: *Coombe Cellars*; smuggling associations.

Combe Martin: *Pack of Cards*; 18th-century inn built like a pack of cards. Press Gang Table inside.

Dartington: *Cott Inn*; 600 year old thatched inn, once a cock fighting centre. Fishing in tarns or on the Dart.

Doddiscombsleigh: *Nobody Inn*; 16th century with ships' timbers.

Exeter: *Double Locks*; Queen Anne building beside the canal, once used by bargemen.

Hackney: *Passage House Inn*; once used by bargemen. Roman site.

Hatherleigh: *George*; 500 year old coach house. At one time a monks' rest-house. Trout and salmon fishing and shooting.

Hope Cove: *Hope and Anchor*; over 700 years old.

Kingsbridge: *Crabshell*: 17th century. Sea fishing.

Knowstone: *Mason's Arms*; 14th-century inn originally built for workers on the church.

Lifton: *Arundell Arms*; old thatched cockpit.

Lundy: *Marisco*; on an island 12½ miles off the coast. Home of political refugees, pirates, smugglers and many wrecked ships.

Lynmouth: *Rising Sun*; 14th-century thatched inn. Secluded fishing.

Lynton: *Crown*; old building originally a village alehouse.

Maidencombe: *Thatched Tavern*; 300 year old thatched cottage, once used by free traders.

Milton Coombe: *Who'd Have Thought It*; 16th century. Reputed to be haunted.

Modbury: *Red Devon*; Queen Elizabeth was entertained here after the Armada.

Plymouth: *Burton Boys*; associated with the Bretons who raided the district often in the 14th and 15th centuries.

Poundsgate: *Tavistock*; 14th-century spiral granite staircase.

Sheepwash: *Half Moon*; salmon, brown trout and sea trout fishing on the Torridge; stocked trout lake; bass fishing at Appledore.

Sourton: *Highwayman*; old coach forms part of the doorway.

South Zeal; *Oxenham Arms*; 12th-century monks' rest house. Built round two granite monoliths. Eggesford Foxhounds and Mid-Devon Foxhounds meet here.

Stoke Gabriel: *Castle*; 600 year old free trading inn with a tunnel leading to the church.

Stokenham: *Tradesman's Arms*; 15th-century cottage inn.

Tavistock: *Cottage Inn*; cellar carved out of rock.

Torbryan: *Church House*; dates from the 14th century. 400 year old set of skittles.

Totnes: *Kingsbridge Inn*; Saxon fireplace of A.D. 900. Charles the Second stayed here.

Umberleigh: *Rising Sun*; previously a priest's house. Now a fishing inn on the Taw.

DORSET

Almer: *World's End*; licensed in 1589. One room covered in signatures.

Charmouth: *George*; Charles the Second stayed here in disguise after the Battle of Worcester.

Corscombe: *Fox*; 350 years old. The bar is of old barrel staves.

Corfe Mullen: *Coventry Arms*; supposedly haunted by a poltergeist. 500 year old skeleton of a crucified cat found in the rafters.

Godmanstone: *Smith's Arms*; smallest inn in England, once the village smithy. Thatched.

DURHAM

Darlington: *Copper Beech*; pigeon lofts used by the fanciers from the local pigeon racing club.

Marsden: *Grotto*; modern inn. Many stories of hermits and smugglers connected with the caves in the cliff face behind.

ESSEX

Braintree: *White Hart*; coaching inn, 400 years old with a yard and gallery.

Chigwell: *Ye Olde King's Head*; large Elizabethan inn.

Hempstead: *Rose and Crown*; Dick Turpin was born here in 1705. 30 foot cockpit across the road.

Ivy Chimneys: *Spotted Dog*; the notorious Waltham Blacks poached here in the 18th century.

Maldon: *Blue Boar*; part 13th century, with a yard.

Saffron Walden: *Rose and Crown*; Shakespeare stayed here more than once.

FIFE

Anstruther: *Smugglers' Inn*; 300 years old. Reservoir and river fishing.

GLOUCESTERSHIRE

Alveston: *Ship*: posting and coaching inn once frequented by smugglers. Connected with cricket and W. G. Grace.

Bisley: *Bear*; once a courthouse. Skittle alley used to be the cellars and is hewn out of rock.

Bristol: *Ye Olde Llandoger Trow*; sailors' inn built in 1664. Often visited by the Press Gang – secret staircase where men escaped from the gangs.

Cherington: *Trouble House*; scene of Civil War fights and 18th-century riots.

Cirencester: *Fleece*; Elizabethan, once used by wool merchants.

Coleford: *Speech House*; first built in 1017 as a Court of Justice. Rebuilt 1676.

Col St. Aldwyn: *New Inn*; once a malt house and a beer house.

Filkins: *Lamb*; old inn of Cotswold stone.

Gloucester: *New Inn*; 500 years old, built for pilgrims going to the shrine of Edward the Second.

Gretton: *Royal Oak*; previously a cheese house and a cider house.

Moreton-in-Marsh: *White Hart Royal*; 16th century with a cobbled courtyard. Charles the First stayed here.

Painswick: *Falcon*; 16th-century inn with an old bowling green.

GLOUCESTERSHIRE continued

St. John's Bridge: *Trout Inn*; 700 years old, on the Thames.

Tetbury: *Lamb*; once a meeting place for Jacobites.

Tewkesbury: *Gupshill Manor*; 14th-century timbered inn.

Winchcombe: *George*; 700 year old rest-house for pilgrims. Stone bath used by the pilgrims can still be seen.

Withington: *Mill*; mentioned in the Domesday Book.

HAMPSHIRE

Beaulieu: *Montagu Arms*; 12th century.

Beauworth: *Fox and Hounds*; built in King Stephen's reign. Contains a 300 foot well and a large tread wheel.

Bucklers Hard: *Master Builders House*; established in the 18th century.

Crondall: *Plume of Feathers;* 12th-century coaching inn.

Eversley Cross: *Chequers*; cricket is played on the village green opposite.

Farnborough: *Tumbledown Dick*; Dick Turpin visited this inn.

Godshill: *Fighting Cocks*; cockfighting ring in the village green opposite.

Hamble: *Bugle*; very ancient building, possibly 12th century.

Hambledon: *New Inn*; home of cricket.

Holbury: *Old Mill*; 11th-century thatched inn, said to be haunted.

Hurstbourne Tarrant: *George and Dragon*; associated with William Cobbett.

Liphook: *Royal Anchor*; large coaching house dating from *c.* 1745. Edward the Second, Queen Anne, Samuel Pepys, Nelson all slept here at various times.

Lymington: *King's Head*; cobbled forecourt. Once a centre of smuggling.

Odiham: *King's Arms*; 14th-century timber framed inn.

Pilley: *Fleur-de-Lys*; oldest inn in the New Forest.

Rockford Green: *Alice Lisle Inn*; named after Dame Alice Lisle who was executed in 1685 at Winchester.

Romsey: *White Horse*; Tudor inn once a rest-house connected with the Norman Abbey.

Southampton: *Red Lion*; Henry the Fifth's cousin, Earl of Cambridge, was tried and beheaded here before Agincourt.

Stockbridge: *Grosvenor*; on the Test. Trout fishing and horse racing inn.

Tiptoe: *Plough*; *c.* 1700, with cob walls. Near Lymington.

HEREFORDSHIRE

Hereford: *Black Lion*; old house with some interesting 16th-century murals.

Ledbury: *Feathers*: build in 1521. Assembly Room supported by pillars over the stable yard.

Pembridge: *New Inn*; half-timbered inn with projecting gables. Once a court house. The treaty ending the Wars of the Roses signed here.

HERTFORDSHIRE

Ayot St. Lawrence: *Brocket Arms*; 14th-century inn with a passage to the church once used by monks.

Berkhamsted: *King's Arms*; old posting inn. Archery used to be practised in the garden.

Broadwater: *Roebuck*; gabled inn built in 1420.

Broxbourne: *Crown*; old angling inn where quoits is still played.

Chipperfield: *Two Brewers*; old timber inn with a courtyard. The prizefighters Bob Fitzsimmons, Jem Mace, Sayers and others trained here.

Cromer Hyde: *Chequers*; Regency inn.

Hitchin: *Sun*; old coaching and posting inn of the 16th century. Secret room in one of the bedrooms. Malt and brew houses in the gardens.

Much Hadham: *Red Lion*; 15th century. One of the fireplaces opens on to a secret staircase.

St. Albans: *Fighting Cocks*; one of England's oldest inns. Octagonal building. Oliver Cromwell slept here. A tunnel runs to the monastery nearby.

Stevenage: *Castle*; Henry Trigg, 18th-century landlord, made a will that he be placed in a coffin in the stable. It is still there.

Tewin: *Rose and Crown*; the building next door was once a skittle alley.

Welwyn: *White Hart*; Lord Melbourne held private race meetings here.

HUNTINGDONSHIRE

Huntingdon: *George*; posting and coaching inn with a yard and a gallery. Pike and perch fishing in the Ouse.

INVERNESS-SHIRE

Fort Augustus: *Lovat Arms*; part of the old fort (built 1654) still stands in the grounds. Salmon and trout fishing.
Invergarry: *Glengarry Castle*; Invergarry Castle lies in the grounds. Salmon and trout fishing. Stalking.
Kingcraig: *Suie*; fishing on Loch Insh and Spey. Stuffed capercailzies on show.
Nr. Loch Ness: *Flichity Inn*; trout fishing on Loch Ruthven. On the south side of Loch Ness.
Lynwilg: *Lynwilg Inn*; fishing on Loch Alvie and Tay.
Newtonmore: *Balavil Arms*; fishing, rough-shooting and deerstalking.
Whitebridge: *Whitebridge Inn*; brown trout, salmon and sea trout fishing on various lochs including Loch Ness.

ISLE OF WIGHT

Cowes: *Gloster*; Victorian inn. Verandah like a ship's quarterdeck.

KENT

Bidenham: *Three Chimneys*; previously a guard house for French prisoners in the 19th century.
Bluebell Hill: *Robin Hood*; 600 years old.
Brenchley: *Rose and Crown*; 14th-century house converted from stables.
Broadstairs: *Royal Albion*; *c.* 1800. Connected with Dickens.
Bromley: *Downham Tavern*; largest inn in England.
Plough; old coaching inn. Skittles, quoits, dominoes, and tippit still played here.
Brookland: *Woolpack*; 15th century.
Canterbury: *Brewers Delight*; pike, perch and roach fishing. Bat and Trap played here.
Falstaff; 650 years old. Used by pilgrims.
Chilham: *White Horse*; haunted by a vicar who killed himself here several centuries ago. Associations with Wat Tyler's rebels.
Cranbrook: *George*; Great Court Room where French prisoners were tried.
Detling: *Cock Horse*; 14th-century coaching inn on the Pilgrims' Way.
Dymchurch: *Ship*; smuggling centre with secret staircases and hiding places.
Egerton: *George*; old inn with ships' timbers.
Fairbourne Heath: *Pepper Box*; converted from a slaughterhouse.
Folkestone: *True Briton*; boxing inn, frequented by many famous fighters. Also renowned for its dart players.
Fordcombe: *Chafford Arms*; stoolball is still played here.
Goudhurst: *Peacock*; 14th-century free trading inn.
Herne Bay: *King Ethelbert*; wildfowling area.
Hernhill: *Red Lion*; 14th-century pilgrims' rest-house.
Langley Green: *Dr. Samuel Johnson*; marble-playing inn.
Sandwich: *Bell*; posting and coaching inn with an Assembly Room and musicians' Gallery.
Sarre: *Crown*; nearly five centuries old. Many connections with smugglers and highwaymen.
Sheerness: *Royal Fountain*; naval inn of Charles the Second's reign.
Speldhurst: *George and Dragon*; 13th-century timbered inn. Third oldest inn in the country.
Tonbridge: *Cardinal's Error*; originally two 16th-century cottages.

KINROSS

Kinross: *Kirklands Inn*; once a coaching house. Fishing.

KIRKCUDBRIGHTSHIRE

Gatehouse-of-Fleet: *Murray Arms*; old posting and coaching inn. Roughshooting. Fishing on five lochs and the Fleet.

LANCASHIRE

Bolton: *Old Man and Scythe*; half timbered inn built in 1636.
Hale: *Childe of Hale*; so called after a 9 foot 3 inch giant born here in the 16th century.
Hawkeshead: *Drunken Duck*; over 400 years old.
Heaton-with-Oxcliffe: *Golden Ball*; on a 6 foot platform beside the River Lune.

LANCASHIRE continued

Manchester: *Seven Stars*; over 600 years as a licensed house. Once connected by a passage to the church.

Walkden: *Swan with Two Necks*; old inn with village stocks outside.

LEICESTERSHIRE

Bottesford: *Bull*; 14th-century building in Belvoir Vale, a hunting area.

Market Harborough: *Three Swans*; 14th-century inn with a 17th-century sign of wrought iron.

LINCOLNSHIRE

Grantham: *Angel and Royal*; 12th-century hostel for the Knights Templars; later King John held court here.

Spalding: *White Hart*; rebuilt 1714. First records are dated 1377.

LONDON

Aldgate High St., E.C.3: *Hoop and Grapes*; oldest inn in the City, with a tunnel to the Tower. Supposed to be haunted.

Bishopsgate, E.C.2: *Dirty Dick's*; rebuilt 1870. Once a winehouse, still has wine vaults.

Catherine St., W.C.2: *Nell of Old Drury*; a passage, used by Charles the Second, runs to Drury Lane Theatre.

Charles St., W.1: *Running Footman*; used by 18th-century runners, who ran ahead of noblemen's carriages.

Chingford Hatch, E.4: *Horseless Carriage*; motoring inn with a veteran car on show.

Coldharbour Lane, E.14: *Gun*; beside the river, with many tunnels once used by smugglers. Nelson stayed here.

Deptford: *Prince Regent*; once well known for its trotting matches, now a boxing inn.

Drury Lane: *White Hart*; built 1216. Prisoners from the Tyburn had their last drinks here before going to the gallows.

Ely Place, E.C.1: *Mitre*; once part of Ely Palace where the Bishops of Ely lived. Dated 1546.

Fetter Lane, E.C.4: *Printer's Devil*; associated with the printers of Fleet Street, which is very close.

Fleet St., E.C.4: *Old Bell*; burnt down in the Great Fire and rebuilt by Christopher Wren. Literary associations.

Old Cheshire Cheese; old chop-house burnt down in the Fire of 1666 and rebuilt. Known by Dr. Johnson.

Haverstock Hill, N.W.3: *Noble Art*; boxing inn where many champions have trained.

Highgate Village, N.6: *Flask*; coaching inn of Henry the Sixth's reign. Associated with Dick Turpin.

Jew's Row, S.W.18: *Ship*; Georgian house once renowned for its gambling.

Kew Bridge: *Star and Garter*; well known in the 19th century. Balloon ascents occurred from here.

Knightrider St., E.C.4: *Horn*; ancient inn on the street where the knights once rode to the jousting.

Lower Richmond Rd.: *Fox and Hounds*; Oxford boat race crew trained here for several years.

Ludgate Hill: *Belle Sauvage*; 15th-century coaching inn. Once had stabling for 400 horses.

North End Way, N.W.3: *Old Bull and Bush*; 17th-century farmhouse. Frequented by various literary characters including Dickens.

Old Bailey, E.C.4: *Magpie and Stump*; gallows used to be just outside. Once had a tunnel running to Newgate Prison next door.

Rotherhithe St., S.E.16: *Mayflower*; associated with the Pilgrim Fathers. By the river.

St. Martin-le-Grand: *Bull and Mouth*; coaching inn which once had underground stabling for 700 horses.

St. Martin's Lane, W.C.2: *Salisbury*; Victorian inn famous for its prize fights.

St. Michael's Alley, E.C.3: *Jamaica Wine House*; the first London coffee house. 17th century.

Strand-on-the-Green, W.4: *City Barge*; given a 500 year Charter by Queen Elizabeth.

Upper Mall, W.6: *Doves*; small 17th century inn by the river. Once a well known coffee house.

Upper Richmond Rd., S.W.15: *Coach and Eight*: many rowing associations.

Violet Hill, St. John's Wood: *Abbey*; has its own archery grounds.

Wapping High St., E.1: *Town of Ramsgate*; *c.* 1680 riverside inn. Judge Jeffreys was attacked here by a mob.

Wapping Wall, E.1: *Prospect of Whitby*; built *c.* 1500. Much Press Gang recruiting went on here. Cock-fighting bar and prize fighting ring.

Westbourne Grove: *Alma*; famous for its billiards.

MIDDLESEX

Sipson Green: *Three Magpies*; 16th century. Connections with highwaymen.

Uxbridge: *Crown and Treaty*: built 1575. Conference in the Treaty Room in 1645 between Parliamentarians and Royalists.

MIDLOTHIAN

Duddingston: *Sheep's Heid*; old Scottish howff.

Edinburgh: *Deacon Brodie*; 18th-century tavern once owned by a deacon who turned out to be a notorious robber and was hanged.

MONMOUTHSHIRE

Abergavenny: *Angel*; posting and coaching inn on the site of a monastery.

Monmouth: *King's Head*; coaching inn built in the reign of Henry the Fifth.

Raglan: *Beaufort Arms*; supposedly tunnels lead from the church to the inn cellars.

MONTGOMERY

Mallwyd: *Brigands Inn*; 15th-century coaching inn. Lake trout fishing. River salmon and sea-trout fishing.

MORAYSHIRE

Elgin: *Gordon Arms*; fishing in the Spey estuary. Shooting.

Fochabers: *Gordon Arms*; 19th-century coaching house. Fishing and shooting.

Forres: *Queen's Head*; old inn with fishing on three lochs.

NORFOLK

Bradwell-Juxta-Mare: smuggling associations. In 1860 32 guns shot nearly 1,000 brent-geese here in one night.

Harleston: *Swan*; coaching inn with a panelled Assembly Room.

Hickling: *Pleasure Boat*; pike fishing and duck shooting.

Mundford: *Crown*; Falconry Club once met here. Shooting and coursing.

Norwich: *Bell*; pre 1600. Cockfighting centre. Old gallery.

Scole: *Scole Inn*; 17th century coaching and posting inn famous for its sign across the road.

Thetford: *Bell*; *c.* 1493. Courtyard and gallery.

NORTHAMPTONSHIRE

Oundle: *Talbot*; 7th century rest-house for the monastery, rebuilt in 1626.

Stoke Bruerne: *Boat*; old thatched inn, once used by bargemen on the Grand Union Canal.

NORTHUMBERLAND

Backworth: *Backworth Inn*; large whippet racing club holds races behind the inn in a field on Sunday mornings.

Corbridge: *Angel*; 16th century coaching inn with a Tudor window. Good salmon fishing.

Cornhill-on-Tweed: *Collingwood Arms*; salmon and trout fishing on the Tweed. North Northumberland and Berwickshire Hunt nearby.

Ponteland: *Black Bird*; 14th century inn.

Shilbottle: *Farriers Arms*; old inn with a long hunting tradition.

Weldon Bridge: *Angler's Arms*; old coaching and fishing inn on the Coquet. The Percy Hunt meet here – they have their own drink, Percy punch.

NOTTINGHAMSHIRE

Nottingham: *Flying Horse*; Tudor building on a very old site. Huge sandstone cellars.

nr. Nottingham: *Trip to Jerusalem*; *c.* 1070. Caves in the cellars, one leading to Nottingham Castle above the inn.

Southwell: *Saracen's Head*; Charles the First surrendered here to the Scots Commissioners in 1646.

OXFORDSHIRE

Burcot: *Chequers*; 16th-century thatched house.

Caulcott: *Horse and Groom*; *c.* 400 years old.

Chipping Norton: *Fox*; farmers' inn near the 'Rollright Stones'.

Dorchester-on-Thames: *George*; once the monks' brew house. Oak timbered courtyard and long gallery.

Goring-on-Thames: *Ye Miller of Mansfield*; trout fishing on the Thames.

Henley-on-Thames: *Old White Hart*; mentioned in 1490. Once a centre of cockfighting and bear baiting.

OXFORDSHIRE continued

Minster Lovell: *Old Swan*; 600 years old. Associated with Richard III.

Newbridge: *Rose Revived*; old toll-house.

Pishill: *Crown*; farmhouse of the 12th century, once a hideout for Jesuit priests.

Shipton-under-Wychwood: *Shaven Crown*; previously a pilgrims' rest house, then a hunting lodge.

PEEBLESHIRE

Howgate: *Old Howgate*; old Scottish howff. Now a modern tavern.

PERTHSHIRE

nr. Aberfeldy: *Weem Inn*; fishing rights on the Tay.

Blair Atholl: *Atholl Arms*; grouse shooting and trout fishing.

Faskally: *Old Faskally House*; trout fishing on Loch Faskally.

Glenshee: *Dalmunzie Inn*; once a shooting lodge. Stalking, grouse shooting, fishing.

Grandtully: *Grandtully Inn*; salmon and trout fishing on the Tay. Ghillies available.

Kenmore: *Kenmore Inn*; old coaching inn. Fishing – ghillies and boats available.

Killin: *Ardeonaig Inn*; trout and salmon fishing.

RADNORSHIRE

Presteign: *Radnorshire Arms*; half timbered 17th-century inn with a bowling green.

ROSS & CROMARTY

Dundonnel: *Dundonnel Inn*; 19th-century inn built following the Clearances.

Nr. Garve: *Aultguish*; old coaching inn on the moors.

ROXBURGHSHIRE

Kelso: *Ednam House*; trout and salmon fishing.

SHROPSHIRE

Ludlow: *Feathers*; Elizabethan inn with panelled rooms and moulded plaster ceilings.

Oswestry: *Wynnstay*; Georgian coaching and posting house with a bowling green. Queen Victoria stayed here.

Shrewsbury: *Lion*; 18th-century coaching and posting inn with an Adam ballroom. Known by Dickens and de Quincey who both stayed here.

SOMERSET

Bicknoller: *Bicknoller Arms*; 15th-century thatched inn with a skittle alley.

Congresbury: *Star*; old staging house with a skittle alley and ballroom.

Dunster: *Luttrell Arms*; built in 15th century for the monastery. 16th-century skittle alley.

Dulverton: *Lion*; stag, fox, hare and otter hunting. Fishing.

East Hornington: *Slab House Inn*; much of the 16th-century building still remains.

Exford: *White Horse*; 16th century. Hunting, fishing and riding.

Holford: *Plough*; part 14th century. West Somerset Foxhounds and Quantock Staghounds meet here.

Langport: *Langport Arms*; 15th-century moulded ceiling. Posting inn.

Litton: *Ye Olde King's Arms*; 15th century. Old shove-ha'penny table.

Norton St. Philip: *George*; monastic guesthouse of 1223. Samuel Pepys dined here.

Shepton Mallet: *King's Arms*; *c.* 1660. Skittle alley.

South Petherton: *Crown*; old fives wall still in good condition, and an old skittle alley, still used, the second largest in Somerset.

Taunton: *Blackbrook*; 1542. Used to be a courthouse.

Wells: *White Hart*; 15th-century coaching inn. Previously belonged to the Dean and Chapter of the Cathedral.

Winsford: *Royal Oak*; old thatched inn on the Exe. Permanent skittle alley outside.

STAFFORDSHIRE

Kingswinford: *Glynne Arms*; very sunken at one end because of a colliery underneath.

Tutbury: *Ye Olde Dog and Partridge*: 15th-century black and white building.

Uttoxeter: *White Hart*; once HQ for Bonnie Prince Charlie.

STIRLINGSHIRE

Drymen: *Winnock*; long low building. Fishing available.

SUFFOLK

Barton Mills: *Bull*; old posting and coaching house with a courtyard; near Newmarket racecourse.
Framlingham: *Crown*; coaching and posting inn, once a court house. Jacobean panelling.
Hoxne: *Swan*; once a monks' rest-house. Spiral staircase.
Ipswich: *Great White Horse*; important coaching and posting inn, mentioned in the 'Pickwick Papers'. George the Second stayed here.
Long Melford: *Bull*; built 1450, with a yard and open galleries.
Newmarket: *White Hart*; old and famous racing inn.
Orford: *King's Head*; a 13th-century inn with a long smuggling history.
Pin Mill: *Butt and Oyster*; once a Naval Court House.
Stonham: *Magpie*; 15th century. Still has a gallows sign across the road.

SURREY

Bagshot: *Jolly Farmer*; once a farmhouse owned by a farmer who was found to be a highwayman and hung outside.
Bletchingley: *Whyte Harte*; 1388. Fishing and shooting.
Chiddingfold: *Crown*; 13th-century pilgrims' rest house.
Cobham: *Cricketers*; old inn with wattle and daub walls.
Horley: *Ye Olde Six Bells*; 15th-century monks' rest house with an old shove-ha'penny table. Fishing.
Oxted: *Old Bell*; 13th-century half timbered pilgrims' rest house on the Pilgrim's Way.
Shere: *White Horse*; 15th century.
South Godstone: *Fox and Hounds*; *c.* 1358. Freetrading HQ.
West Horsley: *Old Barley Mow*; 4 centuries old. Priesthole behind the fireplace.
Witley: *White Hart*; 600 year old hunting lodge.

SUSSEX

Alfriston: *Star*; 13th-century pilgrims' rest-house. Stoolball still played here.
Bucks Green: *Fox*; 16th century with parts dating back to 1490.
Crawley: *George*; gallows sign-post.
Dell Quay: *Crown and Anchor*; over 400 years old. Free traders' hide-out. Ring the bull is still played.
Findon: *Gun*; *c.* 1675. Shooting men used to leave their guns here.
Fittleworth: *Swan*; 600 years old. Fishing.
Goodwood: *Richmond Arms*; 18th-century inn with a cockpit outside.
Hartfield: *Anchor*; 500 year old inn, once a women's workhouse.
Hooe: *Lamb*; smugglers used the small river outside the inn.
Horsham: *Black Horse*; part of the building is an old Corn Exchange.
Lewes: *White Hart*; 18th century. Dungeon cellars.
Midhurst: *Spread Eagle*; Elizabethan hunting lodge with a secret room.
Mill Hamlet: *Crab and Lobster*; 700 years old.
Old Heathfield: *Star*; pilgrims' rest-house with a hatch where horsemen were served.
Pevensey: *New Inn*; 600 years old.
Rusper: *Plough*; 500 years old, once a rest-house owned by nuns.
Rye: *Bell*; built 1420. Free traders' inn.
Shoreham: *Ye Olde Red Lion*; free traders' inn with a cache for hiding men and casks.
Tinsley Green: *Greyhound*; World Marbles Championships held here on Good Friday.

SUTHERLAND

Dornoch: *Dornoch Inn*; fishing. Dominoes and darts played here.
Golspie: *Sutherland Arms*; established 1808 by the Duke of Sutherland as the county's first coaching inn. Fishing.
Loch Naver: *Altnaharra*; sporting inn built in the 19th century as a result of the Clearances.

WARWICKSHIRE

Bubbenhall: *Three Horseshoes*; very old inn; the village is mentioned in the Domesday Book.
Priors Marston: *Holly Bush*; ancient village inn.
Quinton: *Gay Dog*; old inn connected with racing drivers.
College Arms; over 400 years old. Given to Magdalen College by Henry the Seventh.
Shrewley: *Durham Ox*; 1764. Connected with Guy Fawkes.

WARWICKSHIRE continued

Southam: *Old Mint*; 14th century. Charles the First melted down his silver here.

Stratford-upon-Avon: *White Swan*; Shakespeare was born very near this inn. Famous for the Tobit paintings.

Warwick: *Warwick Arms*; coaching and posting inn with two courtyards.

WESTMORLAND

Appleby: *Crown and Cushion*; good fishing nearby on the Eden.

Ruthwaite: *Swan*; associated with John Peel.

Tirril: *Queen's Head*; built 1715. Cellars hewn out of solid rock. Trout fishing.

WILTSHIRE

Avebury: *Red Lion*; thatched 16th-century inn at the centre of the Avebury Stone Circle. 80 foot well inside the building.

Calne: *Lansdowne Arms*; Elizabethan posting inn with an old brew house and stone-mullioned windows.

Corsham: *Methuen Arms*; Tudor and Georgian inn with an old skittle alley and a dove cote. Unusual design on the doorposts.

Lacock: *Angel*; 700 year old timbered inn with overhanging upper storey and stone-mullioned windows.

Salisbury: *Haunch of Venison*; a chop house of 1320.

Sherston: *Rattlebone*; renowned for its connection with John Rattlebone, a brave Saxon knight.

WORCESTERSHIRE

Bretforton: *Fleece*; 500 year old inn, previously a farm-house. Marks on the flagstones to keep witches away.

Broadway: *Lygon Arms*; coaching inn mentioned in 1540 parish register. Charles the First and Cromwell both visited the inn: hunting country.

Elmley Castle: *Queen Elizabeth*; visited by Queen Elizabeth in 1575.

Evesham: *Crown*; 14th-century coaching inn, once a rest-house for Evesham Abbey. 60 foot well in the inn and a tunnel to the Abbey.

Hadley: *Hadley Bowling Green*; Elizabethan inn next door to one of the oldest bowling greens in England.

Ombersley: *Crown and Sandys*; 500 year old building on a 1500 year old site.

Whittington: *Whittington Inn*; built 1310 by the grandfather of Dick Whittington.

Wyre Piddle: *Anchor*; 400 year old inn on the Avon.

YORKSHIRE

Barnsley: *Tollgate*; Arthur Rowe, World Caber Tossing Champion, practises here.

Doncaster: *Turf*; racing inn associated with Lord George Bentinck.

Greenhow: *Miners Arms*; used by workers from the lead mines which date back to Roman times.

Leyburn: *Black Swan*; huge man-trap, once used to catch poachers is on the wall outside.

Sleights: *Plough*; quoits playing centre.

Upper Greetland: *Spring Rock*; Knur and Spell is played here.

Wheldrake: *Alice Hawthorn*: name comes from a renowned locally owned horse.

Yarm: *Garland Ox*; old coaching inn with a concealed cockpit in the attic, used for illegal Mains.

Nr. York: *Little Wonder*; associated with a very famous mare which won the Derby in 1840.